DANIEL**KR**

A Guide to Day-to-Day Québec French

Please Visit the Website at:
http://www.speakquebec.com

Cover illustration: Éric Godin

Speak Québec
ISBN 0-9780755-0-1

Library and Archives Canada

Printed in Canada

Aperio Multimedia, Inc.
239 Rue du St-Sacrement, #303
Montréal, Québec H2Y 1W9
info@aperio.qc.ca

For Mom and Dad...
Who always taught
that the only true boundries
between cultures are those
we ourselves create.

Thanks

S incere thanks to the following persons, without whom this book could not have been created:

Alain Laferrière, Michel Besner, Yves Boudreault, la famille Brossart-Galley (Chantal, Jean-François, Anne-Lise, et Églantine), Corinne et Francis Prévote, Martin Chouinard, Thérèse Bruno, Claude Cajolet, Michel Collet, Virginia Crabbé, Nancy Daoust, Eva Dawson, François DesRochers, François du Monthier, François Dunn, Nicholas Ericson, Martin Faucher, Paul & Stacey Ford & family, André Gauthier, Eric Godin, Claudia Goyette, Amélie Hébert, Jean-Jacques Hermans, Marie-Claude Hudon, Nina Jones, Peter Kreutlein, Jean Lachance, Luc Laprise, Jacques Larue-Langlois, Laurent Lauzon, Sébastien Lavier, Christian Lavoie, Éric Lebel & Sophie Vincelette, Lyne Michaud, Sandra LeMieux, Isabelle LeMieux, Caroline Lévesque, Raymond Lévesque et famille, Nancy Nadeau, Sammy Nelson, Ann Nickner, Scott Rafer, Manuel Rochon, Michael Sheasby & family, Greg Smith & Diane Laflamme, Michael-David Smith & family, Elisabeth Starenkyj, Steven Tabac, Lisa & Michael Taylor & family, Carol Swedlow, Pierre Toussignant, Josée Tremblay, Marie-Josée Turcotte, Raphael Van Lierop, Keiko Watanabe, and Tami Weinberg.

Table of Contents

Forward

Although many works have been published in recent years to help French speakers better understand the many unique words and expressions found in Québec, almost no such resources exist to help English speakers. As any English Canadian or American visitor to the *Province du Québec* will tell you, the dizzying array of of words and phrases particular to the region creates an almost insurmountable barrier to communicating in french – even for those with a strong command of vocabulary and grammar.

The daily language heard in Québec can actually be thought of as a 'superset' of International French – Québecers comfortably use most french words, but also supplant them with several thousand additional words and colloquialisms of their own. While french-speakers worldwide often joke about the great differences between their spoken and written languages, nowhere is this more in evidence than Québec - few of the thousands of differences from International French heard in conversation are ever written down. Québecers proudly point out that a good percentage of this rich, textured language comes from *le vieux Français* – Old French – brought here by the first settlers. This is complemented by a number of words adopted both from the *Inuit* (indigenous northern peoples) and the Native Americans, and also from modern english. These influences combine to form a language that retains all the expansive and artistic nuances found in International French, but is endowed with the rich cultural detail and informality of North-American English as well.

Speak Québec! is designed to be used by english speakers as a practical handbook for understanding *Québécois* – the day-to-day french spoken in Québec. It is also highly valuable for francophones who wish to understand the english equivalents of common colloquialisms. Although by no means a dictionary of officially-recognized "Canadian French", this book is intended to clearly explain the vocabulary and expressions necessary to speak the rich vernacular found in and around the Province of Québec. In this sense, I deliberately make no judgments herein as to things that are technically or grammatically 'correct', seeking instead to provide the real-world picture of the language needed to understand and appreciate the Québécois culture.

The first part of this work provides a brief history of the Québec language, from its origins in *Nouvelle France* and the Amerindian tongues, to its modern-day influences from english. It also provides a clear explanation of differences in grammar and pronunciation from International French. The second part of the book is a dictionary – a lexicon containing two thousand of the words and phrases most commonly heard throughout the Province, and most necessary for understanding.

In this second edition, we strove to include as many ideas and additions as possible. These ideas originated from letters, emails, and even via the book website, **http://www.speakquebec.com**.

The fundamental goal of this book is to open the doors for better communication and cultural exchange between the Québécois people and others, both domestic and abroad. I wish you luck as you unlock the nuances of this tremendously rich and varied language, and hope that this work provides a concrete means of grasping the *joie de vivre* that stands behind one of North America's most unique and undiscovered cultures.

Dan Kraus
August, 2006

A Brief Linguistic History

NOUVELLE-FRANCE (... - 1763)

The evolution of the Québec language actually began far before the arrival of the first Europeans. The Native Americans (*Inuit*) who migrated thousands of years before across the Bering Strait developed – unbeknownst to them – many words that survive in daily Québec parlance to this day. The Native Americans – such as the Micmac, the Cree, and the Outaouais – also had a hand in the development of the modern Québec tongue, as their cultures grew and thrived, and as they developed words for the unique world around them.

The arrival of the first French explorer (Jacques Cartier, in 1534) brought French traditions, language, and culture of the period to Québec. Although Cartier made three separate trips to North America – traveling up the St Lawrence river as far south as Montréal – it was only half a century later, with the founding of Québec in 1608 by Samuel de Champlain, that France had a true foothold in the new world. The quickly blossoming fur trade in Québec brought a rising tide of explorers to the province. With the founding of *Ville Marie* (modern-day Montréal) in 1642, French presence in the colonies increased quickly, and the development of the Province of Québec was afoot.

Although the language used in Québec during this period largely reflected the accent of Paris (whence most of the earliest French settlers came), certain regional groups also brought their particular dialects – Normand, Basque, Flemish, etc. Many of the unique accents and linguistic tendencies identified in Québec today date straight back to this period – and the reign of Louis XIV.

As would be expected, however, these new settlers lacked words for many of the things they encountered in their new world. The fauna, flora, and native culture about them had no equivalents even in rural France, and so these early pioneers began to use the native terms for things particular to their new world. Native American words were adopted for modes of transport, and new items (toboggans, moccasins, etc) that had never before been encountered. The same held true for names of new animals (wapiti, caribou), and fish (achigan, ouananiche), who were simply identified by a phonetic transcription of the Native American names. The name *ouaouaron* – giant frog – in fact, derives directly from the Native American onomatopoeia for the deep bellowing sound the creature makes. A good number of city names in Québec were derived from the Native American names for places – towns such as Chicoutimi, Tadoussac, Natashquan, and others. Many other modern Québec terms also evolved from these early days, drawn from agriculture, fishing, and winter survival.

British Control (1763-1840)

By the mid 18th-century, the gradual arrival of British interests in the new world – and the 13 colonies below – began to have a significant influence on the original French settlers. The inevitable clashes between the two sides began to reflect the almost continuous state of war between their mother countries. The British and French approaches to colonization were notably different, however – whereas the British remained in an essentially urban lifestyle, the French became familiar with the Native Americans, signed treaties with the tribes, and learned their languages. The significant linguistic overlaps with both English and the native tongues increased, and entirely new French words began to appear.

In September of 1759, the armies of British major general James Wolfe and French General Louis Joseph de Montcalm clashed on the Plains of Abraham, just south of the city of Québec. The British victory in this battle, and the fall of the city of Québec to English forces, forever changed the future of *Nouvelle France*. The other major French towns, such as Montréal, surrendered soon after. This victory promulgated the departure of many of the wealthy French and academics; those who did not return to France were on the whole tradesmen, craftsmen, and farmers, who had already put down familial roots in the new world.

Under the Treaty of Paris in 1763, the King of France surrendered the full rights to the territory of Canada to the British Monarchy. This transfer of power opened the doors to a flood of new English-speaking European colonists – who brought with them new ideas, words, and dialects. Many new terms that developed during this period were based on the perception and integration of these new immigrants – words such as *enfirouapé* (a slur of "wrapped in fur") – a pejorative colloquialism for the wealthy English arriving in Quebec City in the post-war years.

Whereas Québec's earliest commerce had been based on fur trading, the evolving social economy of Quebecers began to center increasingly around agriculture. The years that followed the Treaty of Paris were marked by the establishment of the *Seigneurial* system by the British Regime – some 200 separate fiefs of land along the St. Lawrence river, owned by wealthy British landowners, with the land worked principally by the French farmers and tradesmen. These so-called *Habitants* (those who lived and worked on the land) evolved the Québec tongue even further. The harsh winters, and the almost complete dependency on the St. Lawrence River, brought a spirit of strong independence – *un sens debrouillard* – to the culture, and helped evolve a sense of *savoir-faire* that is noticable in Québec even today.

Along with this Seigneural system grew the deep roots of the Catholic theocracy that dominated much of Québec, and its politics, for the century that followed. This religious influence had a marked effect on the language, and brought many religious terms and words into common use.

THE BIRTH OF CANADA (1840–PRESENT)

As the Industrial Revolution sparked the rise of manufacturing, the process of Québec urbanization accelerated, and the previously-rural Francophones began to increasingly answer the call of opportunity close to ports and commerce. By the late 19th century, Montréal had become Canada's premiere industrial center, welcoming also the waves of European immigrants fleeing war in their homelands. Unfortunately, this quick urbanization caused tension between the British and French cultures. English – the traditional language of commerce – was being challenged for the first time as the business language of the province.

The middle of the 20th century marked Québec's transition away from the Catholic theocracy that had effectively ruled its society for a century and a half, and toward a unified and integrated social structure. This "Quiet Revolution" – a sometimes-violent period denoted by a resurgence of pride in Québec's French heritage – marked an increasing Francophone determination to assert their identity, both in Canada and globally. A new sense of unity developed between Francophones, ultimately culminating in the founding of the *Parti Québécois*, and the referedums for the independence of Québec in the years that followed.

The founding of the *Office de la langue Française* in 1961 – a governmental organization instituted to promote use of the French language in the business workplace, and the culture in general - for the first time formalized Québec's intent to define the lingusitic side of its French heritage. In 1969, Pierre Elliot Trudeau's government introduced the *Official Languages Act*, defining both French and English as official languages of Canada, and guaranteed that all government services be made available in both tongues. Québec, on its own initiative, declared itself a bilingual province, and extended these rights at the provincial level as well. In 1977 the Québec government enacted *Bill 101*, declaring French the official language of the province.

Today, the French and English languages co-exist comfortably in Québec. Although French is the official language of the province, many Quebecois are bilingual – communicating freely in both languages.

Pronunciation

The common language spoken in Québec – *Québecois* - is perhaps most typified by its' distinct accent, which is about as different from Parisian French as North American English is from British English. There are about seven major discernable accents throughout the province, ranging from the deep Acadian of the north, to the expansive accent of the Trois-Rivières region, to the curt *patois* spoken near the American border. In general, the further out from the cities you go, the deeper and more historical the accent becomes. A good example of this is the pre-revolutionary "rolled" R sound, which is still heard in some of the more remote regions of Québec.

Sensibly, much of the reason for this historical accent is that the language in Québec did not follow the same evolutionary path as its mother language in France. Modern Québécois is hence a somewhat complicated mix of 16th-century accents combined with tendencies garnered from modern english. There are also many words and phrases that originate directly from accidental slurs of english words and phrases — such as *aldress* (all dressed), *poutine* (put-in), and so on. The resulting language, while pleasing to the ear, can be very difficult to understand. To complicate matters further, Quebecers are reknowned for their tendency to speak very quickly, and often abbreviate or slur words together.

Below we provide an overview of the major differences in pronunciation and grammar between Québécois and International French.

General Pronunciation Tendancies

/a/ becomes /â/ or /ô/

The Québec /a/ is often very deep, and may more or less resemble an /o/ sound:

moi, là → moé, lô
là, je te dis → lô, chte dzi
câlisse → côlisse

/i/ and /è/ become /é/ and /a/

Perhaps the best-known hallmark of the Québec accent, this tendancy directly reflects the standard pronunciation used prior to the French Revolution.

moi → moé
toi → toé
merci → marci
merde → marde
chercher → charcher
couverture → couvart

/e/ becomes /é/

dehors → déhors
bedaine → bédaine
pesant → pésant

/è/ becomes /é/ or /à/

mère → mére; père → pére
frère → frà
j'avais → j'avà
poulet → poulà
vrai → vrà

/ê/ becomes /**AY**/

fête → f<u>AY</u>te
fève → f<u>AY</u>ve

/u/ becomes /eû/ in front of a consonant

bûche → b<u>eû</u>che
il fume → il f<u>eû</u>me

/i/ often becomes /é/ in front of a consonant

mille → m<u>é</u>lle
pipe → p<u>é</u>pe
risque → r<u>é</u>sque
vite → v<u>é</u>te

/ou/ becomes /ô/ in front of a consonant

courte → c<u>ô</u>rte
il pousse → il p<u>ô</u>sse
toute → t<u>ô</u>te

/in/ becomes a nasal /ain/ at the end of words

chemin → chem<u>ain</u>
jardin → jard<u>ain</u>

/i/ is softer

In general, the /i/ sound is pronounced more softly and quickly:

vite → vit
suite → swit

Slurs

/le/ and /la/ become /l'/

Quebecers often drop the /e/ or /a/ from *le* in front of words that start with a consonant, simply slurring the two consonants together.

Le camion → l'camion
La chandelle → l'chandelle
Le tapis → l'tapis

/u/ becomes /i/, and /ou/ becomes /u/

Deeper vowels, such as /u/ and /ou/ are often replaced with sounds more comfortably produced in the front of the mouth:

bas-culotte → bas-kilotte; député → dépité
soulier → sulier; sous-sol → sus-sol

/j/ pronounced as /ch/

The /j/ sound is often truncated, replaced entirely by a /sh/ or /ch/ sound:

je suis → chwee
justifier → chustifier

/re-/ becomes /ar-/

Quebecers sometimes replace the /re-/ at the beginning of words with /ar-/:

revenir → arvenir
refaire → arfaire

… and often completely drop the vowels /i/, /u/, and /ou/, creating a liaison as necessary with the /z/ sound:

arriver → arver

camisole → camzole
mes idées → mezdees

Affriction

Heard very frequently, affrication is the deliberate addition of an /s/ or /z/ sound after a /t/ or /d/ and a /il/y/ or /u/:

Tu dis → tsu dzi
dur → dzur
peinture → peintsure
tunnel → tsunnel

Dipthongs

Long and nasal vowels are often transformed into dipthongs, providing a more open, and sometimes nasal, sound than in International French:

faire → FAY-yure
banque → bawnque

A particularly frequent case of this is the transformation of /or/ into /aor/:

encore → encaor

Clipped Endings

Quebecers often completely drop the ends of words − especially those ending with /re/ and / le/:

genre → /gen/
article → /arteek/
par exemple → /par examp/

A final /r/ is also often transformed simple into an /é/:

tiroir → tiroé
mouchoir → mouchoé

Verbs & Conjugating

The verbs *être* and *avoir* are pronounced quite differently by Quebecers, and are often almost inaudible in quick speech. Below is a table demonstrating English, International French, and common Québec pronunciations:

Être (to be)

English	Int. French	Québec
I am	je suis	/shui/
You are	tu es	/tay/
He/She/It is	il est	/yay/
	elle est	/elay/
	on est	/onay/
We are	nous sommes	(use "on" form instead)
You (*pl.*) are	vous êtes	/vzêt/
They are	ils sont	/iyson/ elles sont /eson/

Avoir (to have)

English	Int. French	Québec
I have	j'ai	/shé/
You have	tu as	/ta/
He, She, It has	il a	/ya/
	elle a	/ela/
	on a	/ona/
We have	nous avons	(use 'on' form instead)
You (pl.) have	vous avez	/vzavé/
They have	ils ont	/ihyon/
	elles ont	/ezon/

Structural Differences

There are a vast number of differences between French and common Québec parlance at the structural level. We summarize here the elements requiring explanation that are most frequently heard in daily conversation.

Double Words

Words can often be doubled for increased effect, especially in the negative:

Sa musique n'est pas fort-fort. – His music isn't really that great.
Je l'aimais pas ben-ben. – I wasn't really that fond of it.

English Usage

Quebecers primarily use English to enhance an idea, or to express an extreme. For example:

C'était vraiment bad. – That was really the worst.

This also holds for well-known English phrases which have not really been appropriated into common usage – if the French word seems overly complex, Quebecers will often simply substitute the English word.

Les Autres

Quebecers often replace *nous* with *nous autres*, and *vous* with *vous âutres*. This is similar in style to English "you guys" or "Y'all" rather than just "you". In the *nous* form, it's about the same as "we all".

Nous and Vous

One of the most confusing issues of usage in Québec is with whom to use the *nous* and *vous* forms of verbs. Different from their Gallic cousins, Quebecers are often significantly less formal, and so frequent use of *vous* is often more of a distancing measure than a politeness, especially among young people. As a general rule, introductions are made using the "vous" form – and then people quickly switch to using "tu".

Supressed Articles

The stand-alone particle *à* is often used to replace *ce*, when making reference to a time already familiar in context, such as *à soir* (this evening) or *à matin* (this morning).

When using *à* (meaning "to"), *dans* or *jusqu'à*, the particle following it is often dropped – for example, *à gare* (*à la gare*), *à prochaine* (*à la prochaine*), *dans maison* (*dans la maison*).

Tenses

Quebecers tend to use the conditional very frequently, especially when ordering or asking for something:

Je prend<u>rais</u> le bœuf — … I'll have the beef (when ordering at a restaurant)

Word-Level Changes

The /tsu/ construct

The addition of /tsu/ causes some of the most complicated combinations in Québécois. At many points in the language, on when asking a question, an additional /tsu/ or /s'tu/ is added. Some of the major idiomatic expressions include:

(Ça) se peut-<u>tsu</u> que… — Could it be that…
<u>t</u>'as-tsu — Do you have…
<u>tu</u> peux-tsu — Can you…
<u>s'tu</u> pour vrai? — Is that for real?

Il and Lui

Québécers often drop particles and pronouns almost completely, or relegate them to their final sound. For example:

Eng.:   I've often said…
Fr. :   Je lui ai souvent dit…
Queb. : *<u>J'y</u> ai souvent dit…*

Eng.:   There are three.
Fr. :   *Il y en a trois.*
Queb. : *<u>Y en</u> a trois.*

Là

Là is used in two different senses — to mean "there" (indicative), and also "now". Often heard is the expression *Là, la* — meaning "As for that…" — or literally, "there, now…"

Ne… pas

In Québécois, either the *ne* or the *pas* can be omitted, and still retain the negative sense of the sentence.

> *Je ne peux répondre au téléphone en ce moment.* — I can't come to the phone right now.
>
> *Je peux pas répondre au téléphone en ce moment.* — I can't come to the phone right now.

Prepositions québécois

Sentences in are often terminated with prepositions — similar to English:

> *Le gars que je sors avec* — The guy (that) I'm going out with (*sl.*).

rather than:

> *Le gars avec qui je sors* — The guy with whom I'm going out.

Swears and Insults

S wears and insults (*jurons*) are used with such grace and flair in Québec that they merit a separate chapter to correctly explain their usage and inflection. This chapter includes an overview of the most important words in this more "colorful" part of the Québec tongue, their meanings, and an idea of usage. The reader is advised to use extreme caution with these words, since — as with oaths in English — they can easily offend people in the wrong context.

The Nouns

Most Québec *jurons* are of religious origin, a historical ramification of the strong religious overtones that dominated the society through the 18th and 19th centuries. As such, most of the *jurons* come from objects from and around the ceremony of the Roman Catholic mass.

Baptême : *n.f.* – Baptism.
Câlisse : *n.m.* – Chalice, cup used for receiving wine in the Roman Catholic mass.
Calvaire : *n.m.* – Calvary, place where Christ was crucified.
Ciboire : *n.m.* – Ciborium, dish used for distributing the host in the Roman Catholic mass.
Crisse : *n.m.* – Christ.
Esprit : *n.m.* – Holy Spirit.
Ostie : *n.m.* – Host, body of Christ in the Roman Catholic mass.
Sacrament : *n.m.* – Sacrament.
Saint Chrem **:** *n.m.* **–** Chrism (holy oil)

Tabarnac : *n.m.* – Tabernacle, place where the host is kept.
Viarge : *n.f.* – Virgin, reference to the Virgin Mary.

Although each of the *jurons* has a different meaning, they are more or less interchangeable from an expletive point of view — when used independently, they all roughly equivocate "*shit!*" or "*goddam!*" in terms of visceral effect.

Typical examples of uses might include:

Crisse qu'y fait frette ! — Shit, it's cold!
Sacrament que ce gars-là est épais ! — Goddamit that guy is an idiot!
Câlisse que j'en ai marre ! — I've goddam well had it!
Ostie que je suis tanné ! – I'm so goddam sick of this!

To express frustration or swear lasciviously, combinations of words are often heard — since they're relatively easy to link together:

Ostie de crisse de Tabarnac !
Ostie de ciboire de calvaire !

The word *ostie* is often addended to sentances for added emphasis, for example:

J'en ai marre, ostie ! — I've goddamwell had it!

Additionally, almost any of the nouns can be used in combination with *être* to describe a state of being angry or upset:

être en tabarnac — to be pissed off
être en câlisse — "   " "   "
être en crisse — " " "   "

Là, je suis vraiment en tabarnac ! — I'm really pissed off right now!
La conversation qu'on a eue m'a mis en beau calvaire. — The conversation we had left me furious.

The Use of *jurons* with the partitive "en" generally means "a lot of":

J'en ai eu de la bouffe en tabarnac – I had one hell of a lot of food.

There are, of course, almost infinite variations of each of the above words, most used to soften the sound. *Câlisse* and *Tabarnac* are the most often changed to these less-offensive versions, roughly equivocating "*Damn!*" or "*Dammit!*" in English:

Câlisse : Câline, Calif, Caltor.
Tabarnac : Tabarnouche, Tabarouette, Tabarslak, Taboire, Barnak, Tabarnane, Tabarnic, Taburn,

Other frequently-heard *petits jurons* — less offensive variants — include:

Calvâsse
Cibolle
Maudit
Maususse
Mautadine
Mautadit
Jériboire
Simonac
Saint-gériboire
Saint-sacrifice
Torrieux

The Adjectives

Almost any of the *jurons* can be used to augment the meaning of a noun, or replace the word *très* (very). Note that the gender of the *juron* is always determined by the word it's modifying:

Ça, c'est <u>une ostie de</u> belle fille ! — That's one damn fine looking girl.

Mon chum est <u>un crisse d'idiot</u> ! — My boyfriend is a goddam idiot!

Oaths, especially *crisse* and *câlisse*, sound stronger when used to modify a noun, as in the above example, than when standing on their own.

The Verbs

Most *jurons* also have verb equivalents.

Se crisser de (quelque chose); Se câlisser de (quelque chose); Se tabarnaker de (quelque chose) — to not give a damn about something.

… and so on. For example:

Je m'en crisse s'il fait froid, je vais quand même aller skier.
I don't give a damn if it's cold, I'm still going skiing.

To increase the effect of the words as verbs even further, the word *contre* to the front of either — *s'en contrecâlisse r, s'en contrecrisser.* For example:

Je m'en contrecâlisse s'il vient avec ou non. — I really don't give a shit if he comes along or not.

Both *câlisser* and *crisser* can also indicate direction, in the sense of throwing or projecting something in a careless manner:

Je vais crisser ça dans les vidanges. — I'm gonna throw it the hell out.
Je vais le câlisser dehors s'il continue de même. — I'm gonna throw him the hell out of here if she keeps on like that.

Dictionary

T o simplify reference, the dictionary part of this book is structured alphabetically according to general Québécois terms, which are then subdivided into the different ways in which each word is commonly used.

- English words are included herein only when a difference in nuance or usage makes a justified distinction from standard English usage, or when the frequency of their use makes their importance worth noting. Words which are essentially equivalent in both languages, such as car parts (*dash*, etc.), or words adopted directly from English (*brunch, shack*) are not included.

- Words included that are International French are denoted by a preceding *Fr.* Such French vocabulary is generally included to help indicate the difference between the Québécois language nuance and that of International French, or to highlight words which are used with uncommon frequency in Québec. The reader should bear in mind that in day-to-day language words are often used in both the International French meaning and that particular to Québec, depending on the context. For example, *partir* – which in International French means simply "to leave", can mean "to leave" *or* "to start" in Québécois.

- Italicized phrases following an entry serve as examples of usage. Those phrases offset with a dot, " ", are idioms or phrases commonly heard in conversation.

- Stars are used to denote strong or offensive terms. A single star (★) indicates something which is a bit impolite, a double star (★★) indicates something rude, and a triple star (★★★) indicates something extremely rude or vulgar which should be avoided.

🔆 Due to the frequency of contractions of International French found in Québec parlance (for example, *ben* rather than *bien*, *betôt* rather than *bientôt*, etc), we have included herein phonetic equivalents of commonly-heard contractions and slurs, to help make them simple to find and understand.

Abbreviations / Conventions Used

angl. – anglicism
cf. – see also
conj. - conjunction
contr. – contraction
Def. – deformation
engl. – English
ex. – example
expl.– expletive
expr. – idiomatic expression
impl.– implies
incl. – including
Fr. – International French
Lit. – literally
orig. – origin
pl. – plural
pron. – pronoun
sim. – similar to
sl. - slang
n. – noun
m.– masculine
f.– feminine

A

À : *Prep. – Fr.* to, at, about..

   à soir – tonight.

   à cause (que) – because.

      C'est pas d'à cause ! – You're right!

   à cette heure (là) – now, at this point. *Lit.* "at this hour".

   à cheval sur les détails – hung up on the details *Lit.* on horseback for the details.

   à date – until now.

   à l'instant – now, at (this) time.

   à mort – to the extreme *Lit.* unto death.

   Il est pénible à mort. – He's unbelivably annoying.

   à part (de) ça – Aside from that, additionally.

   à peine – with difficulty.

(en) Abondance : *n.m.* – a lot (of something).

Abreuvoir : *n.m.* – water fountain, tap.

Abrier : *v.t.* – to cover, to shelter, to protect.

  As-tu abrié tes rosiers ? Ça va geler ce soir. – Did you cover the rosebushes? It's going to freeze tonight.

Accommodations : *n.f. pl.* – lodging, accommodations.

Accoté(e) : *adj.* – hooked, attached.

  Je suis un homme accoté. – I'm an attached man.

   être accoté – to live together (out of wedlock).

Accoter : *v.t.* – 1. to compete with, to challenge. 2. to attain the same level as (the competition)

Accoucher : *v.i.* – to give birth.

> ❧ *Accouche qu'on baptise !* – Get on with it! *Lit.* Give birth so we can baptize! Often only the first word is used, and the rest understood : « *Accouche !* »

Accrocher : *v.t.* – *Fr.* to hang up. 2. to run into, to collide with.

> ❧ *accrocher ses patins* – to end one's career, give up. *Lit.* to hang up [one's] skates.

(d') Accoutumée : *adv.* – typically, usually.

> *D'Accountumée, il arrive vers cinq heures.* – Typically, he arrives around five o'clock.

Achalandé(e) : *adj.* – congested, crowded.

> *La rue était trop achalandée pour faire du vélo.* – The road was too congested to go bike-riding.

Achalage : *n.m.* – annoyance, nonsense.

Achalant(e) : *n.m./f. & adj.* – (one who is) annoying, bothersome, exasperating.

Achaler : *v.t.* – to harass, to annoy, to disturb.

Acharné : *adj.* – insisting, overly forceful. Used when speaking of people, not objects.

Achever : *v.t.* – to make it to the end, to bring to a conclusion.

> ❧ *Il faut qu'il continue à travailler s'il veut achever.* – He needs to keep working if he wants to make it.

Actuellement : *adv.* - currently, presently.

🌿 *La compagnie fait actuellement face à deux défis* – The company is
currently facing two challenges.

Adon : *n.m.* – luck, chance.

On s'est croisés par adon. – We happened to bump into each
other yesterday.
🌿 *Bien d'adon* – willing to get along, willing to help.
Mon prof est bien d'adon quand je lui démande de m'aider avec tout ca
– My professor is really wiling to help when I ask him to give me
a hand with that stuff.

Adonner : *v.i.* – 1. to be convenient, to be possible. 2. to get along (well)

On voulait assister à votre soirée, mais ça n'a pas adonné. – We wanted to
join in your party, but it just wasn't possible.
Ta mère et moi, on s'adonne bien ensemble. – Your mom and I get along great.

Affaire : *n.f.* – 1. thing, item. 2. stuff. 3. issue, problem. 4. business.
5. situation. Not used as *Engl.* "affair", meaning extramarital relationship.

🌿 *faire affaires* – to do business.
🌿 *faire l'affaire* – to be sufficient, to do the job.
Tiens, du savon va faire l'affaire. – Here, some soap will do the job.
🌿 *heures d'affaires* – business hours.
🌿 *paquet d'affaires* – bunch of stuff (to do).
🌿 *(une) drôle d'affaire* – strange situation.
Ramasse tes affaires, s'il te plaît, on s'en va. – Get your stuff together,
please, we're leaving.
C'est pas de mon affaire, mais je pense que t'as tort. – It's none of my
business, but I think you're wrong.
C'est une affaire un peu croche. – It's kind of a nasty deal.

Agace : *n.f.* – *contr.* Agace-pissette.

Agace–pissette★ : *n.f.* – tease (sexual sense).

Agasser : *v.t.* - to bug, to irk, to bother.

Âge d'or : *n.m.* – elderly years. *Lit.* the golden years.

Agrès : *n.m.* – unattractive person.

Aickssa : *expr.* – with that. *Def.* avec ça.

Aiguiller : *v.i.* – to direct, to point (in a direction).

Peux-tu m'aiguiller vers la pharmacie, s'il te plaît ? - Could you point me to to the pharmacy, please?

Aiguiser : *v.t.* – to sharpen.

Aiguisoir : *n.m.*- pencil sharpener.

Aînés : *n.m. pl.* – the elderly.

Ainsi de suite : *conj.* – *Fr.* and so on and so forth.

Air : *n.m.* – 1. *Fr.* air 2. the semblance, the similarity.

- *avoir l'air.* – to seem, to appear.
  Ça a l'air qu'ils y vont quand même. – It seems like they're going anyway.
- *avoir un air de bœuf* - to be in a bad mood.
- *avoir l'air idiot.* – to seem like an idiot.
- *avoir l'air mais pas la chanson.* – to have it in principle, but not in practice. *Lit.* to have the tune but not the song.

Aisé : *adj.* – easy, in a relaxed sense.

    ❄ *prendre (ça) aisé.* – to take it easy.

Ajustable : *adj.* – adjustable.

Âldresse : *adj.* – with everything (sandwich, pizza, etc). *Def. eng.* all-dressed.

Alentour(s) : *n.masc. pl.* – 1. surroundings, local area. 2. around.

Est-ce qu'il y a un dépanneur dans les alentours ? – Is there a convenience store around here?
Il y a plusieurs gamins alentour du char. – There're several kids around the car.

Alldress : *adj.* – with everything. Used in the context of food. *Def. Engl.* all dressed.

Je prends un hamburger alldress, s'il te plaît. – I'll take a hamburger with everything, please.

Aller : *v.i.* – 1. to go. 2. *sl.* to go for, to accept.

Je vais y aller pour le steak aussi. – I'll go for the steak too.
    ❄ *au pire aller* – in the worst case.
    ❄ *aller au batte* – to go to bat (for something or someone), to step up to the plate, to face an upleasant situation.
    ❄ *aller à malle* – to go get the mail.
    ❄ *aller aux vues* – to go to the movies.

Allô : *expr.* – Hello. Often used in the same sense as *Bonjour*, not exclusively on the telephone, as in France.

Allumé : *adj.* – 1. *Fr.* lit, lighted 2. lit, a bit tipsy. 3. (sexually) excited.

Allumer : *v.t., v.i.*– 1. *Fr.* to light up, to illuminate. 2. to become clear or lucid. 3. to excite sexually, *sl.* to turn on.

> *J'ai allumé l'instant qu'il me l'a expliqué.* – I understood the moment he explained it to me.
> *Arrête de m'allumer, toi !* – Stop turning me on!

Allure : *n.f.* – set of desired qualities, allure.

> ❦ *avoir de l'allure* – to be acceptable, good, valuable.
> ❦ *(ne pas) avoir de l'allure* – 1. (of a person) to have bad judgement
> 2. (of a situation) to make no sense.
> *Ça n'a pas d'allure, ta situation.* – Your situation isn't pretty.

Amanché : *adj.* - 1. set, prepared. 2. stacked (for a girl), well-hung (for a guy).

Amancher : *v.t., v.i.* – to be prepared, to be all set.

> *Cette affaire-là est super bien amanchée.* – That business is really well-prepared.
> ❦ *mal amanché* – badly off, unprepared.

Amanchage : see *Amanchure*.

Amanchure : *n.f.* - 1. trouble, mess. 2. badly-done work.

(s') Ambitionner : *v.i.* – to outdo one's self.

Ami(e) : *n.m/f.* – *Fr.* friend.

> ❦ *ami de garçon* – boyfriend.
> ❦ *amie de fille* – girlfriend.

Amour : *n.m.* – *Fr.* Love.

> ❦ *tomber en amour* – to fall in love.

An? : *expr.* – huh?

Anglo : *n.m.* – *contr.* anglophone.

Anglophone : *n.m/f* – native English-speaker.

Anniversaire : *n.f.* – anniversary (marriage, etc.). Note that in Québec the word *fête*, rather than *anniversaire*, is the word generally used for 'birthday'.

Annonce(s) : *n.f. pl.* – public message(s), commercial(s).

Je vais y aller pendant les annonces. – I'll go during a commercial.

Anweille (donc)! : *expr.* – *sl.* C'mon! Move your butt! *Def. Envoye donc!*

Anteka : *expr.* – anyhow, in any case. *Def.* En tout cas.

Aouair : *v.t.* – to have. *Def.* avoir.

On va aouair un méchant fun à soir. – We'll have a wicked good time tonight.

Appel : *n.m.* – call, phone call.

 appel à frais virés – collect call.
 placer un appel – to place a call.

Applaudissement(s) : *n.m.* – clapping, cheers.

Appui-livres : *n.m.* – Pl. bookends.

Après : *prep.* – 1. after, afterwards. 2. against.

Je vais la voir après. – I'm going to see her afterwards.
Elle est fâchée après lui. – She's mad at him.
 par après – afterwards, next.

Armoire : *n.f.* – 1. cupboard. 2. closet.

Arracher : *v.t.* –1. to tear, to rip. 2. to have difficulty doing something.

    être en arrache – to be out of money; to be broke.
       Ma sœur en arrache en ce moment avec son cours d'Anglais. – My sister
       is really having problems in her English class right now.
    arracher le cœur – to be terribly upsetting. *Lit.* 'to tear the heart'.

Arranger : *v.t.* – to set up, to arrange.

    Je t'ai arrangé un souper avec mon ami. – I set up a dinner for you with
    my friend.
    arranger le cadran (de quelqu'un) – to beat (someone) up. *Lit.* to set
    (someone's) alarm clock.

Arriver : *v.i.* – *Fr.* to arrive.

    arriver comme un chien dans un jeu de quilles - to come crashing into a
    situation. *Lit.* to arrive like a dog into a bowling game.

Arrêt : *n.m.* – 1. stop. 2. stop sign. Most Québec stopsigns are uniqely
written with *ARRÊT,* rather than STOP.

Arsoudre : *v.i.* – *Def. resoudre* (to arrive uninvited)

Arsuer : *v.i.* – to fog up (a mirror, window, etc)

Arvenir : *v.i.* – *Def. revenir* (to come back).

Arvirer : *v.i.* – *Def. revirer* (to turn around).

Arvoler : *v.i.* – *Def. revoler* (to fly apart).

Assermentation : *n.f.* – swearing-in (ceremony).

(s')Assir : *v.i.* – *Def. s'asseoir* (to sit).

Astheure : *expr.* – Now, nowadays. *Def.* À cette heure.

Astiner : *v.i.* – cf. Ostiner.

Astineux(-euse) : *n.m/f & adj.* - cf. Ostineux

Atacas : *n.m. pl.* – cranberry (jelly).

Atchoum : *n.m.* – sneeze.

Atchoumer : *v.i.* – to sneeze. From the onomatopoeia (« *Atchoo !* »).

Atteignable : *adj.* – attainable, able to be achieved.

Attendre : *v.i.* – *Fr.* to wait, to stay.

- *attendre aprés (quelqu'un)* – to wait for (someone).
- *attendre minute* – hold on a sec.
- *attendre du nouveau* – to be expecting a child; to be pregnant
  Lit. to wait for a new one.

Attention à toi ! : *expr.* - Take care of yourself!

Attraper : *v.t., v.i.* – *Fr.* to catch.

- *attraper son air* – 1. to catch one's breath 2. to be caught by surprise
  by something or someone.

Au juste : *expr.* – anyway, actually.

- *C'est quoi ça, au juste ?* – What is that, anyway?

Aubaine : *n.f.* – sale, discount.

Autant (que) : *adv.* – as much (as).

  (En) autant que… – insofar as…

Autoroute : *n.f.* – highway. Highways in Québec are often referred to simply by their number – *Ex.* « la 40 » (Autoroute 40), « la 112 » (autoroute 112), etc.

Autre : *adj.* – *Fr.* other, further.

　✂ *... ou autre* – ... or something else.

Avant-midi : *n.m.* – morning. *Lit.* before-noon.

Avec : 1. *Fr.* with. 2. also.

　✂ *Dérangez-vous pas, on va aller avec.* – Don't worry, we'll go also.

Avoir : *v.t., v.i.* – *Fr.* to have.

　Il n'y a rien là. – don't sweat it, it's nothing, it's not important.
　✂ *(se faire) avoir* – to be had, to be taken advantage of.
　✂ *avoir l'air* – to seem.
　✂ *avoir l'air de la chienne à Jacques* – to be badly dressed. *Lit.* to seem like Jacques' dog.
　✂ *avoir l'air simple* – to make a fool of oneself.
　✂ *avoir un air de bœuf* - to be in a bad mood.
　✂ *avoir un face de bœuf* – to be in a bad mood. *Lit.* to have a face of beef.
　✂ *avoir les baguettes en l'air* – to gesticulate wildly.
　✂ *avoir des bébittes* - to have problems/issues. *Lit.* to have bugs.
　✂ *avoir des bidous* – to have money, to be rich.
　✂ *avoir les bleus* – to be down in the dumps, to have the blues.
　✂ *avoir sa botte* – to be involved in a sexual relationship.
　✂ *avoir son biscuit* – to have one's proper compensation.
　✂ *avoir de la broue dans le toupet* – to have much work to do.
　✂ *avoir le cerveau en marmelade* – to be all mixed up. *Lit.* to have jelly for brains.

- *avoir du chien* – to have determination or character. *Lit.* to have some dog.
- *avoir le gros bout du bâton* – to have the advantage. *Lit.* to hold the big end of the stick.
- *avoir du chiendent* – to have a lot of character.
- *avoir la chienne* – to be afraid, to be worried.
- *avoir le cœur dans la gorge* – 1. to be nauseous. 2. to be on the verge of tears. *Lit.* to have one's heart in one's throat.
- *avoir la couenne dure* – to be thick-skinned.
- *avoir un coup dans le nez* – to have drunk a lot.
- *avoir juste le cul et les dents* – 1. to have no personality. 2. to be extremely thin. *Lit.* to have just an ass and teeth.
- *avoir la coupe rude* – to be in a bad mood. *Lit.* 'to have a rude cut'.
- *avoir la face à terre* – to be annoyed, to be vexed.
- *avoir la falle basse* - to have a long face, to be down.
- *avoir la felle creuse* – to be very hungry.
- *avoir de la classe* – to have class, to be educated. Generally used in the negative, to describe someone (« *Pas de classe !* »).
- *avoir une crotte sur le cœur* – to have a chip on one's shoulder, to be prejudiced against someone.
- *avoir le feu au cul*★★ – to be furious. *Lit.* to have fire in one's ass.
- *avoir le feu au passage* – to be furious. *Lit.* to have fire in the passage.
- *avoir un front de beu* – to be unflappable, to be unshakable. *Lit.* to have the brow of an ox.
- *avoir du fun* – to have fun, to have a good time.
- *avoir le goût (de faire quelque chose)* – to feel like (doing something).
- *avoir des gosses*★ – *sl.* to have balls, to be brave.
- *avoir de la gueule* – to have character, to have a strong presence. *Lit.* to have mouth.
- *avoir la gueule fendue jusqu'aux oreilles* – to be grinning from ear to ear.
- *avoir du guts* – *sl.* to have guts.

* *avoir des idées croches* – to have bad (dishonest) thoughts.
* *avoir de la jarnigoine* – 1. to be a chatterbox, to be overly talkative. 2. to be intelligent.
* *avoir un kick sur quelqu'un* – to have a crush on someone.
* *avoir la langue à terre* – 1. to be exhausted. 2. to be very hungry. *Lit.* to have (one's) tongue on the ground.
* *avoir la langue sale* – to have a dirty mouth. *Lit.* to have a dirty tongue.
* *avoir les mains pleines de pouces* – to be all thumbs.
* *avoir la mèche courte* – to have a short fuse, to be quick-tempered.
* *avoir de la mine dans le crayon* – to have a ravenous sexual appetite *Lit.* to have lead in the pencil.
* *avoir de la misère* – to have difficulty.
* *avoir le moton* – to be choked up, to have a lump in one's throat.
* *avoir le motton* – to have bucks, to have money.
* *avoir le nez brun* – to be a brown-noser.
* *avoir les oreilles dans le crin* – 1. to be careful, fearing something or someone. 2. to be in a bad mood. *Lit.* to have one's ears in horse-hair.
* *avoir les deux pieds dans la même bottine* – to be clumsy, unresourceful. *Lit.* to have both feet in the same shoe.
* *avoir une poignée dans le dos* – to be gullible. *Lit.* to have a handle on one's back.
* *avoir quelque chose pour une chanson* – to get something for a song.
* *avoir le sourire fendu jusqu'aux oreilles* – to be smiling from ear to ear.
* *avoir le temps dans sa poche* – to take one's time, to go slowly. *Lit.* to have time in one's pocket.
* *avoir la tête à Papineau* – to be very intelligent. *Lit.* to have the head of Papineau.
* *avoir le va-vite* – to have diarrhea. *Lit.* to have the go-quickly.
* *avoir de la visite* – to have guests (over).
* *avoir son voyage* – to have had enough, to be fed up. *Lit.* to have one's trip.
* *avoir vu neiger* – to have experience. *Lit.* to have seen it snow before.

❧ *avoir des yeux (tout) croches* – to have squinty eyes.

❧ *avoir les yeux dans le beurre* – to be tired.

❧ *avoir les deux yeux dans le même trou* – to be exhausted. *impl.* to be staring at a point in space. *Lit.* to have both one's eyes in the same hole.

❧ *avoir des yeux pochés* – to have rings around one's eyes.

❧ *avoir des yeux rond comme des piastres* – to have eyes round like saucers.

❧ *avoir des yeux tout le tour de la tête* – to have eyes in the back of one's head.

Ayoye ! : *excl.* – 1. Ouch! 2. Wow!

B

Babillard : *n.m.* – billboard.

Baboune : *n.f.* – *Fr.* lips.

❧ *faire la baboune* – to pout.

Backer : *v.t., v.i.* – to back up, support (financially or otherwise).

On a trouvé quelqu'un pour backer notre nouvelle business. – We found someone to support us in our new business.

Backstore : *n.m.* – storage, backroom.

Bacon : *n.m.* – 1. Bacon, ham. 2. Money, cash.

Sors ton bacon, ça va coûter cher ! – Get out your money, this is going to cost quite a bit!

❧ *se pogner le bacon* – to goof off, to do nothing

Bad : *adj.* – *Eng.* (extremely) bad. Used to imply the worst possible case.

C'est vraiment bad, son problème. – His problem is really the worst.

Badloqué : *adj.* – unlucky.

Bâdrant(e) : *adj.* – annoying, irritating.

Bâdrer : *v.t.* – to bother, annoy.

   Ne me bâdre pas avec tes histoires. – Don't bother me with your tales.

Badtripper : *v.i.* – 1. to flip out, to be distracted 2. to suffer 3. to have a bad trip (drug-related)

   Elle badtrippe depuis le mort de son père.– She's been a mess since her dad died.

(se) Baigner : *v.t./v.i.* – to bathe

   ❦ *baigner dans l'huile* – to go well, to go smoothly. *Lit.* to bathe in oil.

Bagosse : *n.f.* – alcohol.

Bain : *n.m.* – bath, bathtub.

   ❦ *bain tourbillon* – whirlpool, hottub.

Bajoues : *n.f. pl.* – rosy cheeks.

Bal des finissants : *n.m.* – prom.

Balai : *n.m.* – broom.

   ❦ *ballon-balai* – broom-ball. Popular Québec game derived from hockey, played on–foot using brooms and a ball rather than sticks and a puck.
   ❦ *fou comme un balai* – overjoyed, exuberant. *Lit.* crazy as a broom.

Balance : *n.f.* – 1. *Fr.* scale. 2. balance (financial term).

Voici le moitié, je te paierai la balance demain. – Here's half, I'll give you the balance tomorrow.

Balancigner : *v.i.* – to balance on a see-saw.

Les gamins veulent aller balancigner dans le parc – The kids want to to go see-saw in the park.

Balayeuse (électrique) : *n.f.* – vacuum.

Veux-tu passer la balayeuse dans le salon, s'il te plaît ? – Would you vacuum the living room, please?

Ballone : *n.f.* – balloon.

❧ *être en balloune* – to be pregnant.
❧ *partir sur une balloune* – to go on a bender, to get drunk.
❧ *souffler dans la balloune.* – to take a breathalyzer test. *Lit.* to blow in the balloon.

Balle : *n.f.* – ball. Often used to denote a responsibility, as in English.

Ouais, il m'a passé la balle là-dessus. – Yeah, he passed me the ball on that.

Baloné : *n.m.* – baloney.

Banc de neige : *n.m. /expr.* – snowbank.

Baptême★★ : *excl.* – Shit! ★★ *Lit.* Baptism.

Barbier : *n.m.* – barber (for men).

Barbot : *n.m.* – drawings, markings, graffiti.

Barda : *n.m.* – noise

  ❄ *faire du barda* – to be noisy.

Barfer : *v.i.* – to barf, to throw up.

Barré(e) : *n.m.* – barred, kept out.

  On risque d'être barrés d'ici si tu continues de même. – We are going to be thrown out of here permanently if you keep that up.

Barginer : *v.t.* – to deal, to bargain.

  Il s'est barginé un super de bon deal. – He bargained himself a great deal.

Barniques : *n.f. pl.* – glasses, spectacles.

Barre : *n.f.* – bar.

  ❄ *barre de savon* – bar of soap.

Barré : *adj.* – locked.

Barrer : *v.t.* – to lock.

  As-tu barré la porte ? – Did you lock the door?

Barrure : *n.f.* – lock, deadbolt.

Bas : *adj.*– *Fr.* low.

  ❄ *en bas de…* – below…

Bâs : *n.m.* – socks, stockings.

  ❄ *manger (ses) bâs* – to be uncomfortable with one's speech or action, *sim.* "open mouth, extract foot". *Lit.* to eat one's socks.

Bas–culottes : *n.m. pl.* – panty-hose.

(se) Batâiller : *v.i.* – to argue, to dispute.

Bâtisse : *n.f.* – building.

Bâton : n.m. – stick, club.

  ❧ *avoir le gros boutte du bâton* – to have the advantage *Lit.* to hold the big end of the stick).

Bat : *n.m.* – 1. bat. (baseball). 2. Joint (marijuana)

  ❧ *aller au bat* – to go to bat for something or someone, *i.e.* to face an upleasant situation.

Bavassage : *n.m.* – gossip.

Bavasser : *v.i.* – to gossip, to talk behind someone's back.

Bavasseux (-euse) : *n.m/f* – gossipy person.

Baveux, euse : n. *& adj.* – arrogant, annoying, offensive (person)

Bazou : *adj.* – jalopy, heap.

  ❧ *Aye, c'est un beau bazou, ça !* – Hey, nice car!

Beau/belle : *adj.* – *Fr.* beautiful, nice.

  ❧ *C'est beau.* – It's nice/good. Often used in reply to thanks.
  ❧ *beau smatte* – wise-ass, smarty-pants.

Bébé la-la : *n.m.* – one who acts like a child; crybaby.

Bébelle : *n.f.* – 1. toy. 2. thing, small object.

  Ramasse tes bébelles, on s'en va, là. – Pick up your toys, we're leaving now.

Bébitte : *n.m.* – insect.

- *avoir des bébittes* – to have problems/issues.
- *bébite à patates* – ladybug.

Bec : *n.m.* – small kiss, especially the double-cheek kiss popular in Québec.

- *bec sucré* – sweet tooth.
- *faire le bec fin* – to be fussy about what one eats.
- *se sucrer le bec* – to eat, particularly sweets.

Bécosse : *n.f.* – bathroom, toilet. *Contr.* engl. Back-house.

- *aller aux bécosses* – to go to the bathroom.

Bedaine : *n.m.* – belly, *sl.* gut.

- *bedaine de bière* – beer-belly.
- *se promener en bedaine* – to go shirtless.
  Aye, tu commences à avoir une vraie bedaine, là ! – Hey, you're starting to get a real gut!

Ben : *adj., adv.* – well. *Contr.* bien.

- *ben-ben* – very.
  Ce n'était pas ben-ben bon, finalement – It wasn't that great, after all.
- ben manque – probably, perhaps.
  On va ben manque aller souper ensemble ce soir – We'll probably dine together tonight.

Benefic : *adj.* – beneficial, advantageous.

Bémol : *n.m.* – negative thing, negative idea.

Il y a juste un petit bémol : Jacques ne vient pas. – There's just one negative thing – Jacques won't be coming.

Bécher : *v.t.* – to fall, to trip on something.

Bequer : *v.t.* – to kiss, to give a peck.

Bétail : *n.m.* – 1. beast (of burden). 2. difficult job or task.

   ostie** *de bétail* – a hell of a job.

Bête : *adj.* – rude, impolite.

   avoir l'air bête – to seem unfriendly.
   faire un air bête – to look (at someone) with contempt.

Bête puante : *n.m.* – skunk.

Bêtise : *n.f.* – 1. *Fr.* Nonsense, silliness. 2. insult, affront.

Béton : *n.m.* – *Fr.* concrete.

   couler (quelque chose) dans le béton – to write (something) in stone, to fix something permanently. *Lit.* to pour something in concrete.

Betôt : *adv* – soon (*contr.* bientôt).

Bette : *n.f.* – beet, face.

   Lui as-tu vu la bette quand on l'a trouvé? – Did you see his face when we found him?

Beurre : *n.m.* – *Fr.* butter.

   avoir les yeux dans le beurre – to be tired.
   beurre de pinotte – peanut butter.
   pédaler dans le beurre – to make useless efforts.

Beurrer : *v.t.* – *Fr.* to butter, to spread.

   beurrer épais – to lay it on thick, to exaggerate.

❄ *beurrer la face* – to show someone up, to rub something in someone else's face.

Jean m'a beurré la face avec son nouveau travail. – Jean rubbed his new job in my face.

Beus : *n.m. pl.* – police, *sl.* cops, pigs. *Contr.* French *bœufs* (steer, oxen).

Biberon : *n.m.* – *Fr.* baby bottle

❄ *boire comme un biberon* – to drink like a fish.

Bibitte : *n.f.* – 1. insect. 2. problem, issue.

❄ *avoir des bibittes* – to have problems.
❄ *Bibitte à poil* – small animal.
❄ *Bibitte à patates* – cockroach.

Bicycle à gaz : *n.m.* – motorcycle.

Bidou : *n.m.* – money.

❄ *avoir des bidous* – to have money, to be well-off.

Bien-être social : *n.m.* – welfare. Abbreviated as *BS*.

Bienvenue ! : *expr.* – Welcome! Also used in response to "Thanks" ("You're welcome").

Bière : *n.f.* – *Fr.* beer.

❄ *bière d'épinette* – root beer.
❄ *bière en fût* – draft beer.
❄ *bière tablette* – room–temperature beer.
❄ *être de la petite bière* – to be without importance. *Lit.* to be of small beer.

Bine : *n.f.* – face.

⚜ *avoir un drôle de bine* - to make a funny face, to make a strange expression.
En goutant sa bière, il a fait un drôle de bine. – When he tasted his beer, he made a funny face.

Binette : *n.f.* – face.

⚜ *avoir un drôle de binette* - to make a funny face, to make a strange expression.
⚜ *En goutant sa bière, il a fait un drôle de binette.* – When he tasted his beer, he made a funny face.

Binnes : *n.m. pl.* – (baked) beans.

⚜ *avoir des yeux dans la graisse de binnes* – 1. to be wiped out, to be exhausted. 2. to be captivated or distracted (by something),
A chaque fois qu'il la voit, il a les deux yeux dans la graisse de binnes – Every time he sees her, he get completely distracted.

Binerie : *n.f.* – small, inexpensive restaurant.

Bisouner : *v.i.* – to fiddle.

Bitcher★★ : *v.t.* – to complain, *sl.* to bitch★★.

Lui, il t'a bitché pendant un bon 10 minutes. – He complained about you for a good 10 minutes.

Bizoune★★ : *n.f.* – sexual organs. Usually male, but occasionally used for the female.

Blanc : *n.m.* **–** blank (space).

⚜ *avoir un blanc de mémoire* – to draw a blank (speaking of one's memory).

Blanchon : *n.m.* – baby seal.

Blé d'Inde : *n.m.* – corn on the cob.

Bleacher : *v.t.* – to bleach, tint white.

> *Demain, je vais me bleacher les cheveux.* – Tomorrow I'm going to bleach my hair.

Bleu : *n.m.* – 1. bruise. 2. state of being sad.

> *J'ai toujours quelques bleus de ma randonnée à bicyclette.* – I still have a few bruises from my bike trip.
>
> *avoir les bleus* – to be down in the dumps, to have the blues.

Bleuet : *n.m.* – 1. blueberry. 2. Native of the Saguenay/Lac-Saint-Jean region, well-known for its blueberries.

Blind pig : *expr.* – Speak-easy, illegal barroom.

Bloc : *n.m.* – 1. city block 2. concrete or other support block.

> *La gare est à trois blocs par là.* – The train station is three blocks that way.
> *Son char est sur les blocs depuis une semaine.* – His car has been up on blocks for one week now.

Bloke★★ : *n.m.* – English Canadian (pejorative).

Blonde : *n.f.* – girlfriend.

Blouse : *n.f.* – woman's shirt, blouse.

Bobettes : *n.f.* – underwear, slip.

Boboche : *n.f.* – (badly-made) object or item.

Bœuf : *n.m.* – 1. *Fr.* Steer 2. *Fr.* pig, cop, police officer.

- *avoir un air de bœuf* - to be in a bad mood.
- *avoir un face de bœuf* - to be in a bad mood.

Boire : *v.t., v.t.* – *Fr.* to drink.

- *boire comme une éponge* – to drink like a sponge.
- *boire du fort* – to drink alcohol. *Lit.* to drink some strong [stuff]).
- *boire comme un biberon* – to drink like a fish. *Lit.* to drink like a baby's bottle.
- *boire comme un trou* – to drink like a fish. *Lit.* to drink like a hole.

Bois : *n.m.* – wood, woods.

- *bois franc* – hardwood.
- *bois mou* – soft wood.
- *sortir du bois* – to make it out of the woods, to escape trouble.
  Il a presque fini, mais il n'est pas encore sorti du bois. – He's almost done, but he's not out of the woods yet.

Boisé : *n.m.* – wooded area, glade.

Boisson : *n.f.* – *Fr.* drink.

- *de la boisson* – (any) alcoholic drink.
- *être en boisson* – to be drunk.

Boîte : *n.f.* – *Fr.* box.

- *boîte à malle* – mailbox.
- *boîte à lunch* – lunchbox.

Bolle : *n.f.* – intelligent person.

Bombe : *n.f.* – kettle.

Bompers : *n.m. pl.* – 1. bumpers (of a car, etc). 2. boobs, breasts.

Bon Jack : *n.m.* – a good fellow, a forthright person.

(le) Bon vieux temps : *expr.* – *Fr.* the good old days.

Bonjour : *expr.* – Good Day. Used both as a greeting and a farewell.

Bonjour, là – See you, now!

Booker : *v.t.* – to schedule, to book.

Je vais booker une salle pour demain. – I'll book a room for tomorrow.

Booster : *v.t., v.t.* – 1. to provide moral support. 2. to jump–start a car.

J'ai besoin des câbles pour booster mon char. – I need cables so I can jump-start my car.

Bord : *n.m.* – side.

Sur le bord de la maison – On the other side of the house.

Bosser : *v.t.* – to boss around, to play the head honcho. Used differently from French *bosser*, meaning "to work".

Lui, il n'arrête pas de bosser tout le monde. – He keeps pushing everybody around.

Botchage : *n.m.* – badly-done work.

Botcher : *v.t.* – to mess up, to botch, *sl.* to screw up.

Botte : *n.f.* – *Fr.* boot. 2. screw.

- *prendre une botte*★★★ – to screw, to have sex with.
- *(une) bonne botte*★★★ – a good screw, a good lay.
- *soule comme une botte* – completely wasted, inebriated. *Lit.* as drunk as a boot.

Bottines : *n.f. pl.* – shoes, footwear.

Boucane : *n.f.* – smoke.

Boucaner : *v.t., v.i.* – to smoke.

Boucher : *v.t.* – 1. *Fr.* to stop up, to close. 2. to shut up.

Il s'est fait boucher pas longtemps après. – He was forced to shut up not long afterwards.

Bouette : *n.f.* – mud, mire.

Bougonneux(euse) : *adj.* – grumpy.

Bouilli : *n.m.* – stew with meat and vegetables, similar to French *pot-au-feu*.

Bougrine : *n.f.* – overcoat, outerwear.

Boules★★ : *n.f. pl.* – *sl.* boobs, breasts.

Bouleversant(e) : *adj.* – staggering, bewildering, incredible.

On a eu des nouvelles bouleversantes ce soir. – We had staggering news this evening.

Bouleverser : *v.t.* – to shock, *sl.* to bowl over, *sl.* to blow away.

Les nouvelles m'ont pas mal bouleversé. – The news shook me quite a bit.

Bourrasser : *v.t.* – to be sharp, rude, bothersome.

Bourratif (-ive) : *adj.* - filling. (food)

Bourré : *adj.* – full (of food).

Bourse : *n.f.* – purse, handbag.

Bout(te) : *n.m.* 1. *Fr.* end, goal. 2. piece or part of something. 3. a while, a period of time.

> ✂ *au boutte* – 1. to the extreme. 2. to the end. 3. really good.
> *Il l'a fait au boutte.* – He did it right up to the end.
> *Il est au boutte, ton char !* – Your car is the greatest!
> *Je l'ai fait pour un boutte.* – I did it for a while.
> ✂ *avoir le gros boutte du bâton* ⸗ to have the advantage *Lit.* to hold the big end of the stick).
> ✂ *faire un boutte* – to leave, to depart, to blow out of (somewhere).
> ✂ *sur le bout de la langue* – on the tip of (one's) tongue.

Boyau : *n.m.* – hose.

> ✂ *boyau d'arrosage* – watering hose.

Brailler : *v.t.* – to cry.

Braillage : *n.m.* – crying, weeping.

Braker : *v.t.* – to brake, to slow down.

Brancher : *v.t.* – 1. *Fr.* to plug-in. 2. to decide, to make up (one's) mind.

Branchez-vous, les amis ! – Make up your minds, guys!

Branler : *v.t.* – to hesitate, take one's time.

> ✂ *branler dans le manche* – to hesitate when making a decision. *Lit.* to hesitate in the handle.

Branleux(euse) : *n.m. /fem. & adj.* – one who is indecisive or hesitant.

Braoule : *n.f.* – large serving spoon.

Bras : *n.m. – Fr.* arm.

- *coûter un bras* – to cost an arm (and a leg).
- *sur le bras* – free, at no cost.

Brassière : *n.m. –* bra.

Break : *n.m. –* break.

- *prendre un break* – 1. to take a break. 2. to stop dating someone temporarily (romantic sense).

Bretelles : *n.f. pl. –* suspenders, braces.

- *(se) péter les bretelles* – to boast, to brag *Lit.* to snap one's suspenders.

Bretter : *v.t. –* 1. to dawdle , to waste time. 2. to drag on, to continue without end.

Arrête de bretter et viens donc avec moi ! – Stop wasting time and c'mon with me!

Breuvage : *n.m. –* beverage, drink.

Brisé(e) : *adj. –* 1. *Fr.* broken, out of order, malfunctioning. 2. depressed, down (for a person).

Broche : *n.f. –* 1. *Fr.* (steel-wire) staple. 2. (wire) pin.

- *broche à foin* – 1. a haywire (thing or person), something out of order. 2. bailing wire. *Lit.* hay staple.

Brocher : *v.t. – Fr.* to staple, attach.

Brocheuse : *n.f.. – Fr.* stapler.

Brosse : *n.f.* – *Fr.* brush, hairbrush.

    prendre une brosse – to go on a bender, to get drunk.

    virer une brosse – to go on a bender, to get drunk.

Broue : *n.f.* – suds, foam.

    avoir de la broue dans le toupet – to have much work to do.

    faire de la broue – to blow hot air, to talk big.

Brûlement : *n.m.* – burning sensation.

(se) Brûler : *v.i.* – to burn one's self (out).

Je me suis vraiment brûlé pour livrer ca à temps – I really burned myself out to deliver that on time.

Brûlot : *n.m.* – mosquito.

Brunante : *n.f.* – sunset, sundown.

Buanderie : *n.f.* – laundromat.

Bûche : *n.f.* – *Fr.* log.

    se tirer une bûche – to join in (a conversation, etc). *Lit.* to pull up a log.

Bûcher : *v.t.* – 1. to fell trees, to log. 2. to work hard.

Bucker : *v.t.* – to buck, to counter (something).

Bumper : *v.t.* – to move (something) out of the way, to bump.

    se faire bumper –, to be downgraded to be pushed out.

Bummer : *v.t., v.t.* – 1. to beg, bum (money). 2. to hang around.

Il avait du monde qui bummait du change dehors. – There were people bumming change outside.

Butin : *n.m.* – clothes.

Buzzant : *adj.* - impressive, amazing.

C

Ça : *pron.* – *Fr.* this, that.

- ❦ *Ça, là…* – And as for that…
- ❦ *Ça doit.* – That must be the case.
- ❦ *C'est ça qui est ça.* – Things will be as they are.
- ❦ *Ça fait que…* – so, therefore. *Lit.* This makes it such that….

Ça va (tu) bien? : *expr.* - 1. How are you doing? 2. Are you OK?

Cabane : *n.f.* – *Fr.* cabin, wood shack.

- ❦ *cabane à sucre* – sugar shack - a cabin in the woods once used in the production of maple syrup, and converted into a restaurant serving traditional Québec foodstuffs.

Cabaret : *n.m.* – tray.

Le serveur a rangé les assiettes sur son cabaret. – The waiter placed the plates on his tray.

Cachette : *n.f.* – hide-and-go-seek game.

- ❦ *jouer à la cachette* – to play hide-and-go-seek.

Cadran : *n.m.* – alarm clock.

Cailler : *v.i.* – to fall asleep.

Caler : *v.t.* – 1. to drink quickly, swallow at a draught, *sl.* chug. 2. to drown.

Vas-y, cale ! – C'mon, drink up!

Câler : *v.t.* – to order, to call.

   ✄ *câler (son) bluff* – to call (someone's) bluff.

   ✄ *câler l'orignal* – to puke, to throw up. *Lit.* to call the moose.

     On a déjà câlé trois pintes de bière. – We already ordered three pints of beer.

Câline★ : *expl.* – Dammit! (gentler form of *câlisse*).

Câlique★ : *expl.* – Dammit! (gentler form of *câlisse*).

Câlisse★★ : *expl.* – Goddamn! *Lit.* "chalice" from the Roman Catholic mass.

Câlisser★★ : *v.i., v.t.* – 1. to leave, to abandon. 2. to not care.

Je m'en câlisse★★ : I don't give a damn.

   ✄ *câlisser (quelqu'un) dehors* – to throw (someone) out.

   ✄ *câlisser une volée* – to beat (someone) up.

Câlissement★ : *adv.* – Goddam.

Calorifère : *n.m.* – *Fr.* electric heater (radiator).

Caltor★ : *expl.* – Dammit! (gentler form of *câlisse*.)

Calvaire★★ : *expl.* – Goddam *Lit.* "Calvary", where Christ was crucified).

Camion : *n.m.* – *Fr.* truck.

   ✄ *camion de vidanges* – garbage truck.

Camionneur : *n.m.* – *Fr.* truck-driver, trucker.

Camisole : *n.f.* – woman's jumper, underwear.

Camp : *n.m.* – camp, camping place.

   ❧ *sacrer son camp* – to leave, to head out.

Canal : *n.m.* – channel, television station.

Canard : *n.m.* - kettle

Canceller : *v.t.* – to cancel, nullify.

Cancer : *n.m.* – old car, *sl.* rusted heap.

Cannone :– *adj.* – striking, highly attractive (woman).

Canisse : *n.f.* – 1. milk drum. 2. can (of soda, beer, etc.).

Canter : *v.i.* – to fall asleep.

Cap de roue : *n.m.* – hubcap.

Capable (de) : *adj.* – 1. *Fr.* able, capable of (something). 2. to stand, to put up with.

   ❧ *Lui, là, je suis pas capable.* – I really can't stand that guy.

Capot : *n.m.* – winter coat.

   ❧ *capot de poil* – fur coat.

Capotant : *adj.* – unbelievable, phenomenal.

Capoté : *adj.* – crazy, out of control, *sl.* nuts.

Capoter : *v.t.* – to lose it, to go crazy, to get carried away.

Oui, j'ai vu ce film-là, ça m'a fait capoter ! – Yes, I saw that film – it made me completely lose it!

   capoter (bien) raide – to panic, to lose one's head.

Carré : *n.m.* – park, square.

   Carré Saint-Louis – Saint Louis Square.

Carreauté(e) : *adj.* – checked, checkered.

Il a mis un chandail carreauté. – He put on a checkered shirt.

Carrément : *adv. expr.* – *Fr.* frankly, honestly. *Lit.* squarely.

Je suis carrément crevé ! – Frankly, I'm bushed!

Carrosse : *n.m.* – carriage, baby carriage.

Cartable : *n.m.* – binder, notebook.

Carte : *n.f.* – 1. *Fr.* card. 2. *Fr.* map.

   mettre (un endroit) sur la carte – to put (someplace) on the map.

Carter : *v.i.* – to card (someone) to verify their age.

Carte-soleil : *n.f.* – Québec health insurance card.

Cas : *n.m.* – *Fr.* case, situation.

   en tout cas – in any case, anyhow.

Cash : *n.m.* – 1. cash (money). 2. cash register.

S'il vous plaît, passez au cash après. – Please go to the checkout counter afterwards.

   passer au cash – to pay the price, to pay one's debt.

Casque : *n.m. – Fr.* hat.

> *(en) avoir plein son casque* – to have enough. *Lit.* to have one's hat full.
> *casque de poil – n.f.* – fur hat.

Cassé : *adj.* – 1. *Fr.* broken. 2. out of money, *sl.* broke.

> *cassé comme un clou* – completely broke. *Lit.* broke as a nail.

Casse-croûte : *n.m.* – Small snack restaurant, often found on the roadside in rural Québec.

Casse-tête : *n.m.* – puzzle. *Lit.* head breaker.

Casser : *v.i.* – 1. *Fr.* to break. 2. to break up, to split up.

> *Ils ont cassé il y a trois semaines environ.* – They broke up about three weeks ago.
> *casser la croûte* – to grab a bite. *Lit.* to break a crust.

Casseux(euse) de party : *n.m.* – bore, *sl.* party-pooper.

Catalogne : *n.f.* – quilt.

Catcher : *v.t.* – to catch on, to get it, to understand.

> *J'ai pas tout catché.* – I didn't get it all.

Catin : *n.m./f.* – 1. *Fr.* doll. 2. prostitute.

Cause : *n.f. – Fr.* reason, cause.

> *à cause que…* – because.

Cave : *adj., n.m./f.* – moron, stupid individual.

Cédule : *n.f.* – schedule, timeline.

Céduler : *v.t.* – to schedule, arrange a time for something.

CEGEP : *n.m.* – Québec junior college.

Cellulaire : *n.m.* – cellular phone.

Cenne : *n.f.* – cent, penny.

J'ai plus une cenne ! – I don't have a cent left!

Centre d'achats : *n.m.* – mall, shopping center.

Cervelle : *n.f.* – *Fr.* brain, head, *sl.* noggin.

Je ne sais pas comment faire rentrer cette idée dans sa cervelle. – I don't know how to get that idea into his noggin.

C'est en plein ça : *expr.* – That's exactly it.

Chaise berçante : *n.f.* – rocking chair.

Chambalant(e) : *adj.*- rickety, unstable.

Chambre de bain : *n.f.* – bathroom.

Champ : *n.m.* – *Fr.* field.

être dans le champ - to be in error, to be mistaken. *Lit.* to be in the field.

Champlure : *n.m.* – faucet, tap.

Chanceux(euse) : *n.m./fem.* & *adj.* – *Fr.* one who is lucky.

Chandail : *n.m.* – long–sleeve shirt, sweater.

Change : *n.m.* – coinage, loose change, spare change.

> *prendre tout son petit change* – to take a tremendous effort. *Lit.* to take all one's spare change.

Changer : *v.t., v.i.* – *Fr.* to change.

> *changer d'idée* – 1. to change (one's) mind. 2. to take a break.
> *changer d'air* – to change one's mood or state of mind.
> *Il doit changer d'air s'il veut s'amuser ce soir.* – He needs to change his state of mind if he wants to have fun tonight.
> *changer quatre trente sous pour une piastre* – 1. to make no profit. 2. to change one thing for another of identical value. *Lit.* to change thirty cents for a quarter.

Chansonnier : *n.m.* – singer/song-writer.

Chanter : *v.t., v.i.* – *Fr.* to sing

> *chanter la pomme* – to flirt. *Lit.* to sing the apple.

Char : *n.m.* – automobile, truck.

> *char de police* – police car.

Charger : *v.t.* – to charge, to bill.

> *Combien tu charges pour celui–là ?* – How much do you charge for this one?

Charge renversée : *expr.* – collect (telephone call).

Châroéyer : *v.t.* – (professional) transporter.

Charrue : *n.f.* – snowplow.

Châssis : *n.m.* – 1. window. 2. window pane.

Chat : *n.f.* – *Fr.* cat.

    Il n'y a pas un chat. – There's no one (there).

    chat sauvage – raccoon.

Chaud : *adj.* – 1. *Fr.* hot, warm. 2. tipsy, slightly drunk.

Chaudasse : *adj.* – tipsy, slightly drunk.

Chaudière : *n.f.* – 1. bucket, metal pail. 2. lunchbox.

Chaudron : *n.m* – cookpot.

Chauffer : *v.t., v.i.* – 1. *Fr.* to warm. 2. to drive.

    Tasse-toué, je veux chauffer un peu. – Move over, I want to drive for a bit.

    chauffer les fesses – to give a spanking. *Lit.* to warm the buttocks.

Chauffrette : *n.f.* – portable (electric) heater.

Chaumière : *n.f.* – *Fr.* cottage, country house.

Chaussettes : *n.f. pl.* – slippers.

Checker : *v.t.* – 1. to verify. 2. to keep an eye on, to guard. 3. to check out, to look at.

    Je vais checker voir. – I'll check and see.

    Peux–tu checker mes bagages pour deux secondes ? – Can you keep an eye on my bags for a few seconds?

    Checke la fille là-bas ! – Check out that girl over there!

Chemin : *n.m.* – *Fr.* path, road, way.

    chemin de garnotte – gravel road.

    chemin de gravelle – gravel road.

Chèque de voyage : *n.f* – traveller's check.

Chevreuil : *n.m.* – deer, buck.

Chez : *prep.* – at the home of (someone). Québécers almost always use the plural form (chez nous, chez vous, chez eux), even when speaking about a residence with only one person

J'm'en va chez nous. – I'm going back to my place.

Chiâleux(euse) : *adj.* & *n.m./fem.* – grumpy, crabby, ill – tempered.

Chiâler : *v.i.* – to complain, *sl.* to bitch. *N.B.* In France this word implies crying or weeping, not complaining.

Chiard : *n.m.* – 1. beef stew. 2. difficulty, complex issue.

   être dans un beau chiard – to be in trouble. *Lit.* to be in a nice stew.

Chicane : *n.f.* – argument, dispute.

   pogner une chicane – to have an argument.

Chicoter : *v.i.* – to bother, to disturb.

Ça m'a chicoté toute la nuit. – It bothered me all night long.

Chien : *adj.* – 1. *Fr.(n.)* dog. 2. chicken, fraidy-cat. 3. mean (person)

Il pourrait, mais il est trop chien pour le faire – He could, but he's too afraid to do it.

   avoir du chien – to have determination or character. Lit. to have some dog.

   son chien est mort (expr) – to be done-in, to be finished. *Lit.* His dog is dead.

Chiendent : *n.m.* – weeds, dog's-tooth grass.

> *avoir du chiendent* – to have a lot of character.

Chienne★★ : *n.f.* – *Fr.* bitch. *Lit.* female dog. A derogatory term for a girl.

> *avoir la chienne* – to be afraid, to be worried.
> *avoir l'air de la chienne à Jacques* – to be badly dressed. *Lit.* to seem like Jacques' dog.

Chier★★★ : *v.t., v.i.* – *Fr.* to shit.

> *Va chier !* – Piss off!
> *Va chier un lunch au large !★★* – Go take a fuckin' hike!
> *chier de l'or en barre★* – to believe oneself to be special. *Lit.* to shit bars of gold.
> *chier dans (ses) culottes★★* – to be afraid, to shit in (one's) pants.
> *Faire chier* – to suck, to be bad.
> *Ça fait chier !* – That sucks!

Chieux : *adj. & n.m./fem.* – scared, coward.

Chigner : *v.i.* – to whine, to snivel.

Chnolles★★ : *n.f.* – balls, testicles.

Chnoute★★ : *n.f.* – shit.

> *Cette affaire-là, c'est juste de la chnoute.* – That thing is just a piece of shit.

Choqué(e) : *adj.* – angry, perturbed.

(se) Choquer : *v.i.* – to become angry.

Chose bine : *pron.* – what's-his-name.

> *Je parlais avec chose bine, là…* – I was talking with what's-his-name…

Chouclaques : *n.m.* – sneakers, running shoes.

Chromo★★ : *n.m.* – troll, ugly person.

Chum : *n.m.* – 1. boyfriend (female referring to male). 2. friend (male referring to male).

 🌿 *être ben chum avec (quelqu'un)* – to be really chummy with (someone)

Chu : *pron.* – *Contr.* Je.

Ciboire : *expl.* – Goddamit!

Cigne : *n.m.* – kitchen sink.

Cimonaque : *expl.* – Dammit!

Cinquante-sous : *n.m* – fifty-cent piece.

Circulaire : *n.f.* – advertisements, junk mail.

 Je reçois constamment des circulaires sous ma porte. – I'm constantly getting advertisements under my door.

Citron : *adj., n.m.* – *Fr.* lemon. Often used as a pejorative word for a car.

 🌿 *se faire passer un citron* – to be handed a lemon.

Clair(e) : *adj.* – clear, lucid.

Clairer : *v.t.* – to clear up, finish, clear out.

 On va clairer de l'espace pour les nouveaux meubles. – We'll make some space for the new furniture.

 🌿 *se faire clairer* – to be thrown out (of a bar, etc.).

Clancher : *v.i.* – 1. to accelerate violently. 2. to work well, *sl.* to take off.

Oui, notre business commence à clancher. – Our business is really starting to take off.

Claques : *n.f. pl.* – rubbers, boots.

Clenche : *n.f.* – latch (of a door, etc.).

Cliquer : *v.i.* – 1. to make sense, *sl.* to click (an idea). 2. to work well.

Je lui ai expliqué cinq fois, mais il n'a pas encore cliqué. – I've explained it to him five times, but it still hasn't clicked.
Ça clique ! – That works!

Clou : *n.m.* – *Fr.* nail.

- *cassé comme un clou* – *sl.* broke, penniless. *Lit.* broke as a nail.
- *cogner des clous* – to be nodding off (to sleep). *Lit.* to drive nails in.
- *tomber comme des clous* – to rain heavily. *Lit.* to fall like nails.

Coche : *n.f.* – groove, cut, notch.

- *monter d'une coche* – to go up a notch.

Cochon(ne) : *adj. & n.m./fem.* – dirty (in a sexual sense). *Lit.* pig-like.

Cocotte : *n.f.* – pine cone.

Code régional : *n.m.* – area code (telephone).

Cœur : *n.m.* – *Fr.* heart.

- *avoir une crotte sur le cœur* – to have a chip on one's shoulder, to be prejudiced against someone.

Coin : *n.m. – Fr.* corner.

> ❧ *tourner les coins ronds* – to steer clear of problems. *Lit.* to turn rounded corners.

Coincé : *adj. & n.m. fem.* – 1. narrow-minded (person) 2. stuck, backed into a corner (literally or figuratively).

> *Ce gars-là, je l'ai toujours trouvé un peu coincé.* – I've always found that guy to be kind've narrow-minded.

Col-bleu : *n.m.* – blue-collar (worker).

Collant : *adj.* – clingy, hanger-on (for a person).

(se) Coller : *v.t., v.i.* – 1. *Fr.* to stick, to glue. 2. to curl up with, to snuggle against.

> ❧ *coller comme la misère sur le pauvre monde* – to be firmly attached to (something). *Lit.* to stick as misery to the poor.

Colleux : *n.m* – 1. hug. 2. clingy person.

Coloc : *n.m. /fem.* – roommate, joint tenant. *Contr.* colocataire.

Colon : *n.m & adj..* – 1. bumpkin, redneck. 2. tasteless, gaudy.

Combines : *n.f. pl.* – long-johns, full-length underwear.

Combler : *vt* – to fill, to provide.

Commande : *n.f.* – order.

> ❧ *faire la commande* – to go (food) shopping.

Comment : *adv.* – 1. *Fr.* how. 2. how much.

> *Comment ça va faire ?* – How much will that be?

Comme : *conj.* – *Fr.* as.

comme quoi que – such that.

Compagnie : *n.f.* – company.

Compléter : *v.t.* – *Fr.* to fill out, complete.

S'il vous plaît, compléter le formulaire – Please fill out the form.

Comprenable : *adj.* – comprehensible, understan-dable.

Comptable agréé : *n.m* – chartered accountant.

Comptant : *adj.* – *Fr.* cash.

🌿 payer comptant – to pay in cash.

Comptoir : *n.m.* – counter.

Je l'ai mis sur le comptoir. – I put it on the counter.

Comté : *n.m.* – county.

Concerné : *adj.* – involved, concerned.

🌿 en autant que je suis concerné – as far as I'm concerned.

Concerner : *v.i.* – to be involved, to be concerned with (something).

En autant que ça me concerne… – Insofar as it involves me…

Confortable : *adj.* – comfortable, at ease.

Congédier : *v.t.* – to fire, to let go of an employee. *Lit.* to vacation.

Conjoint : *n.m.* – life partner.

Connecter : *v.t.* – to connect, plug together.

Conservateur : *n.m./fem. & adj.* – moderate, conser-vative.

(se) Contrecâlisser★★ : *v.i.* – to not give a shit, to not care, to ignore.

Je m'en contrecâlisse s'il vient ou pas. – I don't give a shit if he comes along or not.

(se) Contrecrisser★★ : *v.i.* – to not give a shit, to not care, to ignore.

Je m'en contrecrisse s'il vient ou pas. – I don't give a shit if he comes along or not.

Contrôler : *v.t.* – to control. *N.B.* Different from International French, in which it means "to verify or insure".

Contrôle : *n.m.* – *Fr.* control.

> *sous contrôle* – under control.

Coquelœil *adj.* – blind as a bat.

Coquerelle : *n.f.* – cockroach.

Coqueron : *n.m.* – tiny apartment, *sl.* a closet.

Corde à linge : *n.f.* – washline, clothesline.

> *passer la nuit ur la corde à linge* – to sleep badly. *Lit.* to sleep on the clothesline.

Correct : *adj.* – okay, successful, in order, correct, acceptable.

> *C'est-tu correct?* – Is it ok?

Correspondre : *v.i.* – to contact, to correspond (with someone).

Cossin : *n.m.* – small thing, object.

Costaud : *adj.* **–** stocky, well-built, strong (for a person).

   Peut-être qu'il est petit, mais il est costaud ! – He might be small, but he's built!

Costume de bain : *n.m.* – bathing suit.

Cotation : *n.f.* – quotation, statement of price.

Côtes levées : *n.f. pl.* – spareribs.

Coton : *n.m.* – *Fr.* cotton.

   ✄ *être au coton* – 1. to be at the end of one's means or patience. 2. to be exhausted.
   ✄ *faire coton* – to be pathetic.

(se) Coucher : *v.t.* – *Fr.* to go to bed.

   ✄ *se coucher les fesses à l'air* – to sleep butt-naked. *Lit.* to sleep with one's cheeks to the wind.

Coude : *n.m.* – *Fr.* elbow.

   ✄ *Se lever le coude* – to have several beers. *Lit.* to lift one's elbow.

Coudon : *expr.* – C'mon! *Def.* Ecoute, donc.

Couenne : *n.f.* – skin.

   ✄ *avoir la couenne dure* – to be thick–skinned.

Coulante : *adj.* – slippery (surface, etc).

Couler : *v.i.* – 1. *Fr.* to run, to drip (for a liquid). 2. to blow it, to fail.

Je crois qu'il va encore couler son affaire. – I think he's going to blow it again.

🔹 *couler (quelque chose) dans le béton* – to cast (something) in stone.

Coulisse : *n.f.* – drippings.

Coup : *n.m.* – 1. *Fr.* a drink. 2. a blow.

🔹 *avoir un coup dans le nez* – to have drunk a lot.

🔹 *boire un coup* – to grab a drink.

Il a reçu deux coups à la tête. – He took two blows to the head.

🔹 *coup de fil* – phone call.

🔹 *lâcher un coup de fil* – to give someone a phone call.

Couper : *v.t.* – *Fr.* to cut, to reduce.

🔹 *couper le prix* – to cut the price.

Cour à scrap : *n.m.* – junkyard.

Courâiller : *v.i.* – 1. to chase skirts, to womanize. 2. to run errands.

Courâilleux : *n.m.* – skirt-chaser, womanizer.

Courir : *v.i.* – *Fr.* to run.

🔹 *courir la galipote* – to galivant, to chase women.

Courriel : *n.m.* – electronic mail (email).

Coutellerie : *n.f.* – cutlery, utentils.

Coûter : *v.i.* – *Fr.* to cost.

🔹 *coûter un bras* – to cost an arm (and a leg).

🔹 *couter la peau des fesses* – to cost a fortune. *Lit.* to cost the skin off your butt.

Couvert : *n.m.* – cover, lid.

Couverte : *n.f.* – blanket, cover.

Crampant : *adj.* – funny, hilarious. *Lit.* causing cramps.

Crampé(e) : *adj.* – highly amused. *Lit.* bent in two.

J'étais crampé à cause de ce qu'il a dit. – I was doubled over by what he said.

Crapaud : *adj.* – wily, crafty, untrustworthy.

En affaires, il est crapaud. – In terms of business, he's not very trustworthy.

Crayon : *n.m.* – pen, pencil.

> *avoir de la mine dans le crayon*★ – to have a ravenous sexual appetite.
> *Lit.* to have lead in the pencil.

Cré : *adj.* – "Good old". Used to refer affectionately or ironically to a person, and/or their traits.

Cré Jean, il est venu nous aider ènéouai ! – Good ol' Jean, he came to help us anyway!

Crèche : *n.f.* – orphanage. Whereas *crèche* means "daycare" in France, Québécois generally use *garderie* instead.

Crémage : *n.m.* – icing.

Crère : *v.t., v.i.* – believe. *Def. croire.*

Crée-moi, je suis sincère – I'm not kidding / lying to you.
Il faut me crère ! - You gotta believe me!

Crémage : *n.m.* – icing.

Crème à barbe : *n.f.* – shaving cream.

Crème glacée : *n.f.* – ice cream.

Crémone : *n.f.* – long, knit scarf.

Cretons : *n.m. pl.* – *pâté* made from veal or pork, usually eaten at breakfast.

Creux : *adj.* – 1. *Fr.* deep. 2. far away, isolated.

Crevant(e) : *adj* – hilarious, really funny

C'est un gars crevant – He's a really funny guy.

Criard : *n.m.* – car horn.

Crime ! : *expr.* – Heck!

Crin : *n.m.* – *Fr.* horse–hair.

  avoir les oreilles dans le crin – 1. to be careful, fearing something or someone. 2. to be in a bad mood. *Lit.* to have one's ears in horse-hair.

Crinqué : *adj. & n.m /f.* – pissed off, angry (person).

Crinquer : *v.t.* – to crank, to wind.

Crise : *n.f.* – 1. *Fr.* crisis. 2. fit.

  piquer une crise – to throw a fit. Different from International French in which this means "to faint".

Crisse★★ : *Expl.* – Goddamit. *Lit.* Christ.

  Ben, crisse ! – Oh, hell…

Crissant★ : *adj.* – a pain in the ass.

Crissement★ : *adv.* – (one hell of) a lot

Crisser★ : *v.i.* – 1. to leave. 2. *se crisser de (quelque chose)* – to not give a damn about (something).

> ❧ *crisser dehors* – to throw (someone/something) out.
> ❧ *crisser son camp* – to leave, *sl.* to blow out of somewhere
> ❧ *Je m'en crisse !* – I don't give a damn!
>   *Crisse-moi patience !* – beat it! leave me the heck alone!

Croche : *adj.* – *Fr.* bad, nasty, dishonest.

> ❧ *avoir des idées croches* – to have bad (dishonest) thoughts.
> ❧ *avoir les yeux (tout) croches* – to have squinty eyes.
> ❧ *être tout croche* – 1. to be bad. 2. to be dirty, distasteful. 3. to be hung over.
> ❧ *penser croche* - to think dirty (sexual sense).

(se) Crosser★★★ : *v.i.* – 1. to wank, to masturbate. 2. to counter, to go against.

> ❧ *se faire crosser* – to be screwed over, to be betrayed.
>   *Je ne veux pas me faire crosser là-dessus.* – I don't want to be screwed over on this.

Crosseur(euse)★ : *n.m./fem.* – cheat, traitor, hypocrit.

Cru : *adj.* – *Fr.* raw. Often used to describe the weather (raw & cold).

Cruiser : *v.t.* – 1. to hit on (someone), to make a pass at (someone). 2. to go out cruising.

> *Il n'a pas arrêté de la cruiser toute la soirée.* – He didn't stop hitting on her all night.

Cruising-bar : *expr.* – meat-market , pick-up joint.

Cul : *n.m.* – 1. *Fr.* end. 2. *Fr.* ass★★.

- *avoir juste le cul et les dents* – 1. to have no personality. 2. to be extremely thin. *Lit.* to have just an ass and teeth.
- *avoir le trou de cul en dessous du bras*★★ – to be exhausted. *Lit.* to have one's asshole under the arm.

Culottes : *n.f.* – pants.

- *les culottes à terre* – with (one's) pants down.

D

D'abord : *adv.* – 1. *Fr.* first. 2. already.

Je vais tinker mon char d'abord. – I'm going to fill up my car first.
Dis-moi, d'abord ! – Tell me, already!

- *OK d'abord !* – OK then!
- *d'abord que* – since, given that.
    D'abord que tu y vas, moi j'ai pas besoin. – Since you're going, I don't need to.

Dactylo : *n.m.* – typewriter.

Danse : *n.f.* – *Fr.* dance.

- *Danse carrée* – square dance.

Dash : *n.m.* – dashboard (of a car).

- *fesser dans le dash*– to be surprising, to be unexpected.

De même : *adv.* – like this/that.

Je n'aime pas les gars de même. – I don't like guys like that.

De quoi : *pron.* – something.

Je voudrais bien faire de quoi. – I'd really like to do something.

De suite : *expr.* – right away, immediately.

On va faire ça de suite – We'll do that right away.

Débalancé : *adj.* – out of whack, unbalanced.

Débalancer : *v.t.* – to throw out of whack, to unbalance.

Débarbouillette : *n.f.* – washcloth.

Débarque : *n.f.* – fall.

⚜ *prendre une débarque* – to take a fall.

Débarquer : *v.t., v.i.* – 1. to take down. 2. to exit from a vehicle. 3. to quit.

On est débarqué de son char juste à côté de la piste. – We got out of the car right next to the ski slope.
Tout de même, Jacques va débarquer du conseil d'administration l'année prochaine. – Even so, Jacques will leave the board of directors next year.

Débarrer : *v.t.* – to unlock.

Je viens de débarrer la porte. – I just unlocked the door.

Débâtir : *v.t.* – to demolish, to knock down. *Lit.* to unbuild.

Ils vont débâtir la vieille église demain. – They're going to demolish the old church tomorrow.

Débile : *adj. & n.m.* – awesome, unbelievable, insane. Can be used in a positive or negative sense.

C'est débile, ce film-là ! – That film is just amazing!

Débiné : *adj.* – depressed, demotivated.

Débiner : *v.i.* - to depress, to demotivate.

Sa copine l'a quitté, alors il est mal débiné – His girlfriend left him, so he's pretty depressed.

Décâlissant★ : *adj.* – depressing, a downer.

Décâlissé★ : *adj.* – depressed, down, heartbroken.

Décâlisser★ : *v.t.* – to depress.

Déconcrissé : *adj.* – in pieces, in ruins.

Déconcrisser : *v.t..* – to demolish, to destroy.

Décrissant★ : *adv.* – depressing, a downer.

Décrissé★ : *adj.* – bummed out , disappointed, let down.

Moi, j'étais vraiment décrissé après. – I was really bummed out afterwards.

Décrisser★ : *v.i.* – 1. to beat it, to leave, to depart. 2. to damage, to ruin.

Hé ! décrisse de là ! – Hey you! get the heck outa here!

Décrivable : *adj.* – describable, able to be explained.

Ma situation n'est pas vraiment décrivable. – I can't really describe my situation.

Décrocher : *v.t., v.i.* – 1. *Fr.* to stall, to lose momentum. 2. to fail, give up.

Lui, il décroche encore de l'école. – He's failing in school again.

Décrocheur (-euse) : *n.m/f.* – drop-out.

Dedans : *prep.* – in, within.

🌿 *en dedans que…* – in less than…

Définitivement : *adv.* – definitely, certainly.

(se) Dégréyer : *v.i.* – 1. to take one's coat off, to get undressed. 2. to clear a table after a meal.

Va te dégréyer et reste donc un peu. – Take your coat off and stay a while, then!
Veux-tu me dégrayer la table, s'il te plaît ? – Would you clear the table for me, please?

Dégrincher : *v.t.* – to destroy, to undo.

(se) Déguédiner : *v.i.* – to hurry up, to move quickly.

Déjeuner : *v.i.* – to have breakfast.

Déjeuner : *n.m.* – breakfast. In France *petit-déjeuner* usually implies breakfast, and *déjeuner* implies lunch.

Démancher : *v.t.* – to take off, remove, take down.

Demeurer : *v.i.* – to live, to reside in.

On demeure à Montréal en ce moment. – We live in Montreal right now.

(se) Déniaiser : *v.i.* – to wise up, to smarten up.

Dep : *contr.* – Dépanneur (convenience store).

🌿 *passer au dép.* – swing by the convenience store.

Dépanneur : *n.m.* – 1. convenience store. 2. *Fr.* towing company.

Dépareillé(e) : *adj.* – unique, remarkable.

Dépasser : *v.t.* – 1. *Fr.* to pass. 2. to pass (in a car).

Il n'arrête jamais de dépasser des autos sur l'autoroute. – He never stops passing other cars on the highway.

Dépendamment : *adv.* – depending on, as a function of (something).

Dépeinturer : *v.t.* – to strip, to remove the paint from (something).

Il faut d'abord que je dépeinture le mur. – I have to strip the wall first.

Dépense : *n.f.* – 1. cupboard, cabinet. 2. *Fr.* cost, expenditure.

❧ *au diable la dépense* – to hell with the price. *Lit.* to the devil with the price.

Dépensier(e) : *n.m./fem.* – spendthrift.

Dérangeant(e) : *adj.* – disturbing, bothersome.

Déraincher : *v.t.* – to destroy, to undo.

Dérougir : *v.i.* – to reduce, to diminish, to cease.

Descendre : *v.i, v.t.* – *Fr.* to descend, to go down.

❧ *descendre tous les saints du ciel* – to swear. *Lit.* to bring down all the saints from the heavens.

Désennui : *n.m.* – pastime, diversion, hobby.

Deshe★★★ : *n.f.* – sperm, semen.

Désouffler : *v.t.* – to let the air out (of something).

Détail : *n.m.* – *Fr.* detail, particular.

    ✱ *à cheval sur les détails* – hung up on the details. *Lit.* on horseback about the details.

Déteindu(e) : *adj.* – faded, discolored. *Lit.* un-tinted.

Dévirer : *v.i.* – to turn aside, to change direction.

Diable : *n.m.* – *Fr.* devil.

    ✱ *mener le diable* – to make a racket, cause a disturbance.
    ✱ *tirer le diable par la queue* – to be very poor. *Lit.* to pull the devil by the tail.

D'ici : *conj.* – From now until…

    D'ici un an – within a year.

Différencer : *v.t.* – to distinguish, to tell the difference between (things).

    Moi, je ne peux pas différencer les deux. – I can't tell the two apart.

Dîner : *n.m.* – lunch.

Dîner : *v.i.* – to have lunch.

Disconnecter : *v.t.* – to disconnect, unplug.

Discontinuer : *v.t.* – to discontinue, stop producing.

Dispendieux(euse) : *adj.* – *Fr.* costly, expensive.

Dix cennes : *n.m.* – penny, 10-cent piece.

Dix-huit roues : *n.m.* – 18-wheeler (truck).

Dompe : *n.f.* – dump, waste disposal site.

Domper : *v.t.* – to throw out, to dump.

Donner : *v.t., v.i.* – 1. *Fr.* to give. 2. to seem, to appear (when speaking about the result of something).

    Ça donne le bon effet. – That yields the right effect.

    Ça donne un peu trop compliqué. – That seems a bit complicated.

- *donner la bascule* – traditional Québec birthday practice of grabbing someone by shoulders and ankles and tossing them into the air the same number of times as their age. *Lit.* to give someone the seesaw.
- *donner un bec sur la suce* – to give someone a kiss on the lips.
- *donner le diable à (quelqu'un)* – to give (someone) hell.
- *donner un lift* – to give (someone) a lift.
- *donner de la merde à (quelqu'un)** – to give (someone) shit.
- *donner de la misère à (quelqu'un)* – to give (someone) a hard time.
- *donner du slack à (quelqu'un)* – to give (someone) some slack.
- *donner son 4%* – to send away, to fire. (4% vacation pay, generally reimbursed upon termination of employment).
- *Donnes-y la claque !* – Give it a try!

Dorénavant : *adv.* – *Fr.* henceforth, from this time on.

Dormir : *v.i.* – *Fr. to sleep.*

- *dormir sur la switch* – to waste time, to be slow. *Lit. to sleep on the switch.*
- *dormir au gaz* – to waste time, to be slow. *Lit. to sleep on the gas.*

Dos : *n.m.* – *Fr.* back, rear-side.

- *parler dans le dos de quelqu'un* – to talk behind someone's back.

Douance : *n.f.* – intelligence, qualities of a gifted person.

Doudou : *n.f.* – blanket, comforter.

Douillette : *n.f.* – blanket, comforter.

Down : *n.m.* – period of depression or malcontent.

Après que mon chum m'a quittée, j'ai eu un gros down. – After my boyfriend left me, I was really down for a while.

Down : *adj.* – down, depressed.

Drap : *n.m.* – *Fr.* sheet, curtain.

❦ *être blanc comme un drap* – to be as white as a sheet.

(à) Drette : *n.m.* – 1. *(to the) right. Def. (à) droite.* 2. *straight.*

❦ *drette là* – *right there.*
❦ *tout drette* – *straight ahead.*

Driver : *v.t.* – to be in charge of, to be in control of, to drive.

C'est toi qui vas driver ce projet? – You're the one who will drive this project?

Drôle : *adj.* – 1. *Fr.* funny, amusing 2. funny (strange, weird)

❦ *(une) drôle d'affaire* – strange situation.

Dropper : *v.t.* – 1. to drop, to let go (of something). 2. to plummet downwards.

Je vais le dropper, s'il continue de même. – I'll let him go if he continues like this.

Dû : *adj.* – due, required.

❦ *dû à…* – due to…
❦ *dû pour…* – due for…
Mon char est dû pour un changement d'huile. – My car is due for an oil change.

Dull : *adj.* – boring, dull.

    dull à mourir – deathly boring.

Dumper : *v.t.* – 1. to throw away 2. to drop (someone) off. 3. to break up with (someone)

Ma blonde m'a dumpé il y a trois jours. – My girlfriend dumped me three days ago.

Dur : *adj.* – 1. *Fr.* hard. 2. difficult.

    faire dur – to be in a bad situation or state, to be rough.
    Ça fait un peu dur. – That's kind of a difficult situation.

Durant que : *conj.* – while, during.

E

Eau : *n.f.* – *Fr.* water.

    faire de l'argent comme de l'eau – to make a lot of money. *Lit.* to make money like water.

Écartant : *adj.* – describes an area in which it's easy to become lost.

Écarter : *v.t.* – to lose (something).

J'ai écarté ma montre – I lost my watch.

(s')Écarter : *v.i.* – to become lost.

Je m'écarte chaque fois que je marche dans ce coin-là. – I get lost every time I walk around that area.
Elle est pas mal écarté – She's pretty lost.

Écartillé(e) : *adj.* – with legs spread apart.

Je l'ai trouvé tout écartillé dans la neige. – I found him spread-eagled in the snow.

Échapper : *v.t.* – 1. *Fr.* to escape 2. to drop, to let go.

J'ai échappé mon crayon par terre. – I dropped my pen on the floor.

Échouer : *v.t.* – to fail (a test, etc.).

Écœurant : *adj.* – 1. amazing, phenomenal, out of this world. 2. Disgusting.

C'est un film écœurant ! – It's an amazing film!
Je trouvais son attitude écœurante. – I found his attitude to be disgusting.

Écœurer★ : *v.t.* – to piss off, to bother, to annoy.

Il m'a écœuré toute la nuit, ce gars-là. – That guy annoyed me the whole night.

Écornifler : *v.i.* – to snoop, to peep, to spy on.

Écornifleur(euse) : *n.m./fem.* – snooper, peeping tom.

Écourtiché : *adj.* – very short (for clothes).

Écouter : *v.t.* – 1. *Fr.* to listen. 2. to watch (a film, television, etc.). 3. to obey, to pay attention to.

On a écouté un très bon film hier. – We watched a great film yesterday.
Il faut que tu m'écoutes ! – You have to listen to me!
　 écouter la musique à planche – to listen to very loud music. *Lit.* to listen to music flat-out.

Écrapouti(e) : *adj.* – crushed, collapsed.

Écrapoutir : *v.t.* – to collapse, to breakdown.

(s')Écraser : – *v.t.* – *to crash out, to relax.*

On s'est écrasé sur le divan. – *We crashed out on the sofa.*

Effoirer : *v.t.* – to crush, to flatten.

(s') Effoirer : *v.t.* – to crash out, to collapse.

Après la partie, on s'est effoirés chez lui. – After the party, we crashed at his place.

Effrayant : *adj.* – 1. *Fr.* incredible, disturbing, terrible 2. surprising, incredible, extraordinary.

C'est effrayant comment qu'elle croit tout ce qu'il dit. – It's incredible how she believes everything he says.

Égal : *adv.* – *equally, in equal measure.*

❧ *partager (quelque chose) égal.* – *to split (something) equally.*

Égarouillé(e) : *adj.* – wild, crazed.

Il me regardait avec des yeux égarouillés. – He looked at me with wild eyes.

(s')Éjarrer : *v.i.* – 1. to crash out, to spread out. 2. to attempt to do several things at once (without success).

En arrivant chez moi, j'ai trouvé mon fils éjarré dans le fauteuil. – Upon arriving home, I found my son crashed out on the sofa.

Embarquer : *v.i.* – to get in, get on, join.

Veux-tu embarquer avec moi ? – Do you want to ride with me? (*impl.* in a car).
On va tous embarquer sur le projet ensemble. – We're going to join the project all together.

❧ *embarquer quelqu'un sur le pouce* – to pick up someone hitchhiking.

Embarré(e) : *adj.* – locked in, closed in.

Je me suis fait embarrer au bureau. – I got myself locked in the office.

(pour) Emporter : *v.t.* – to take out, to go.

Je prendrais deux cafés pour emporter, s'il vous plaît. – I'd like two coffees to go, please.

(s')Endormir : *v.t.* – 1. *Fr.* to go to sleep. 2. to be sleepy, to doze off.

Je m'endormais derrière le volant. – I was asleep at the wheel.

Endurer : *v.t.* – to put up with, to endure.

Je ne peux plus l'endurer. – I can't stand him anymore.

Ènéoué : *expr.* – anyway, anyhow. *Def. Eng.* Anyway.

(s')Enfarger : v.i. – 1. to become tangled up in, to get stuck in (something). 2. to trip.

> *s'enfarger dans les fleurs (du tapis)* – to become mired in the details. (*Lit.* to become caught up in the (carpet) flowers).

(se faire) Énfirouaper : *expr.* - to get led along, to get taken.

Enlever : *v.t., v.i.* – *Fr.* to remove, to take off.

> *enlever une pelure* – to remove one's coat *Lit.* to take off a layer.

Engagé(e) : *adj.* – in use, taken.

La ligne est engagée. – The line is busy.

Enmieuter : *v.i.* – to get better, to improve.

Ennuyant(e) : *adj.* – tiring, boring, annoying.

Ennuyeux (euse) : *adj.* – *Fr.* tiring, boring, annoying.

Enregistreuse : *n.f.* – tape recorder.

Enteka : *expr.* – anyhow, in any case. *Def.* En tout cas.

Entre autres : *expr.* – *Among other things.*

Envoye donc! : *expr.* – C'mon, then!

Enwaille (donc)! : *expr.* – *sl.* C'mon! Move your butt! *Def. Envoye donc!*

Épais(se) : *adj. & N. masc/fem.* – 1. thick-skulled (person). 2. fool, idiot, numskull.

   Ce gars là est un épais. – That guy is a numskull.

Épaté : *adj.* – *impressed.*

Épater : *v.t.* – *to impress.*

   épater la gallerie – *to make a grand entrance.*

Épeurant : *adj.* – fear-causing, scary.

Épeurer : *v.t.* – to scare, frighten.

Épicerie : *n.f.* – shop

   faire l'épicerie – to go (food) shopping.

Épingle : *n.f.* – pin, holder.

   épingle à linge – clothespin.

Épinglette : *n.f.* – brooch, pin.

Épivarder : to reprimand, to scold.

(s')Épivarder : *v.i.* – 1. *sl.* to take a breather, to get out a bit. 2. to spread oneself too thin.

Épluchette : *n.f.* – corn-husking party, in which guests husk and cook corn as a part of the festivities.

Épouvantable : *adj.* – atrocious.

Épuisé : *adj.* – *Fr.* burned out, extremely tired.

Escalier roulant : *n.m.* – escalator.

Escousse : *n.f.* – a while, a period of time. *Def. secousse.*

Espérer : *v.i.* – 1. *Fr.* to hope. 2. to wait for.

    Espère-moi sur le coin, j'arrive. – Wait for me on the corner, I'll be right there.

Essence : *n.f.* – flavor, taste.

Estimé : *n.m.* – estimate, price quote.

Étampe : *n.f.* – stamp, symbol.

Étamper : *v.t.* – to stamp.

Étage : *n.m.* – *Fr.* floor, stage. Note that in Québec the first floor of a building is called « *premier étage* », whereas in France it would be called « *rez-de-chaussée* ».

Été des Indiens : *expr.* – Indian summer.

Être : *v.t., v.i.* – to be.

- *être assis sur son steak* – to be in a comfortable financial position. *Lit.* seated upon (one's) steak.
- *être sur le B.S.(Bien-être Social)* – to be on welfare.
- *être en balloune* – to be pregnant.
- *être (bien) blond* – to be dumb. *Lit.* to be (very) blond.
- *être de bonne heure sur le piton* – to be up at the crack of dawn. *Lit.* to be on the button early.
- *être bossu* – to be skilled in business.
- *être sur la brosse* – to be smashed, to be drunk. *Lit.* to be on the brush.
- *être dans le champ* - to be in error, to be mistaken. *Lit.* to be in the field.
- *être ben chum avec (quelqu'un)* – to be really chummy with (someone)
- *être à coté de la track* – to be in error, to make a mistake. *Lit.* to be next to the (train) track.
- *être au coton* – 1. to be at the end of one's means or patience. 2. to be exhausted.
- *être tout croche* – to be bad, to be dirty, to be distasteful.
- *être sur la décrisse★* - to be wrecked, to be in a piteous state.
- *(ne pas) être la fin du monde* – to (not) be the end of the world.
- *être à main* – 1. to be friendly, obliging. 2. to be close, right at hand.
- *être dans le jus* – to be swamped, to be busy. *Lit.* to be in the juice.
- *être dans les patates* – to be in error, to be mistaken. *Lit.* to be in the potatos.
- *être dans la lune* – to be spaced out. *Lit.* to be on the moon.
- *être de la petite bière* – to be without importance. *Lit.* to be of small beer.
- *être en boisson* – to be drunk.
- *être en tabarnac★★* – *sl.* to be pissed off, to be upset.
- *être capable (de)* **–** to be able (to do something).
- *être chaud* – to be drunk, *sl.* to be lit.
- *être en crisse★★* – to be pissed off, to be upset.

🌲 *être en (beau) joualvert* – to be furious

🌲 *être aux femmes*– to be homosexual (for a woman).

🌲 *être game* – to be willing, to be game.

🌲 *être bien gréyé* – to be all set, to be ready.

🌲 *être habillé comme lachienne à Jacques* – to be badly dressed. *Lit.* to be dressed like Jacques' dog.

🌲 *être aux hommes* – to be homosexual (for a man).

🌲 *être mieux de…* – to be better to…

🌲 *être mort de rire* – 1. to be dying (of laughter) 2. to be all set, to be guaranteed success.

🌲 *être né pour un petit pain* – born to be mediocre. *Lit.* to be born for a little bread.

🌲 *être parlable* – to be able to be talked with.

🌲 *être sur le party* – to be in party-mode, to be on a bender.

🌲 *être à pied* – to be in financial difficulty. Opposite sense from English "to be on one's feet" (to be financially independent).

🌲 *être pogné sur (quelqu'un)* – to be stuck on (someone)

🌲 *être pour (quelque chose)* – to be in favor of (something), to be for (something).

🌲 *être dans le rouge* – to be in the red, to be in financial difficulty.

🌲 *être dans le rush* – to be in a rush.

🌲 *être supposé de…* – to be supposed to…

🌲 *être en tabarnac*★★ – to be pissed off, to be upset.

🌲 *être dans le trou* – to be in trouble. *Lit.* to be in a hole

Excusez ! : *expr.* – Excuse me!

Extensionner : *v.t.* – to prolong, to extend.

J'ai fait réparer mon moteur, ça va extensionner un peu combien (de temps) ça dure. – I just had my motor fixed, that should make it last a bit longer.

F

Face : *n.f.* – *Fr.* face, front.

- *avoir la face à terre* – to be annoyed, to be vexed.
- *avoir un face de bœuf* - to be in a bad mood. *Lit.* to have a face of beef.

Fâchant(e) : *adj.* – irritating, annoying, bothersome.

Facture : *n.m.* – bill, tab. *Lit.* invoice.

Faire : *v.i., v.t.* – 1. *Fr.* to do, to make. 2. to seem, to appear.

- *faire l'affaire* – to be sufficient, to do the job.
- *faire un air bête* – to look (at someone) with contempt.
- *faire application* – to apply (*Ex.* for a job).
- *faire de l'argent comme de l'eau* – to make a lot of money *Lit.* to make money like water.
- *faire attention à (quelqu'un)* – take care of (one's) self.
- *se faire avoir* – to be had, to be taken advantage of.
- *faire du barda* – to be noisy.
- *se faire bumper* – to get bumped out, to be pushed aside.
- *faire la baboune* – to pout.
- *faire le bec fin* – to be fussy about what one eats.
- *faire sa bosse* – to make a bundle (of money). *Lit.* to make one's bump.
- *faire le gros bec* – to pout. *Lit.* to make a big face.
- *faire un boute* – *sl.* to blow out of somewhere, to leave, to depart.
- *faire de la broue* – to blow hot air, to talk big. *Lit.* to make suds.
- *faire chier* – to suck, to be bad.
- *faire la commande* – to go (food) shopping.
- *faire coton* – to be pathetic.
- *faire danser les dentiers* – to knock someone's lights out. *Lit.* to make someone's teeth dance.

- *faire le drôle* - to clown around.
- *faire dur* – to be in a bad situation or state, to be rough.
- *(se) faire enfirouaper* – to get screwed over, to get taken.
- *faire l'épicerie* – to go (food) shopping.
- *faire faire (quelque chose)* – to have (something) done.
- *faire fitter* – to adjust.
- *faire la galette* – to make (a lot of) money.
- (se) *faire mettre*★★★ – to get laid, to have sex (with someone).
- *faire à mitaine* – to do by hand. *Lit.* to do by mitten.
- *faire mononcle* – to be old-fashioned, to seem old-fashioned.
- *faire le motton* - to make bucks, to make money.
- *faire opérer* – to make (something) work.
- *faire les cent pas* – to pace (back and forth). *Lit.* to do the hundred paces.
- *faire opérer* – to make (something) function, to make (something) work.
- *faire la palette* – to make a lot of money.
- *faire patate* – to fail. *Lit.* to make potatos.
- *faire patienter* – to make (someone) wait.
- *faire le piastre* – to make bucks, to make a lot of money.
- *faire un pli* – to be bothered or upset by something.
- *(se) faire pleumer* – to get taken, to be had. *Lit.* to get plucked.
- *faire du pouce* – to hitchhike.
- *faire (son) rapport à (quelqu'un)* – to report to (someone).
- *faire une saucette* – to go for a dip (in a pool, etc.).
- *faire semblant* – to pretend.
- *faire du (bon) sens* – to make (good) sense.
- *faire son smatte* – to show off.
- *faire du snow* – to snowboard.
- *(se) faire taper les foufounes* – to get a spanking.
- *faire un téléphone* – to place a call.
- *faire du temps* – to do time (in prison).
- *Fais-toi-s'en pas.* – Don't worry about it.

Je vais le faire faire. – I'm going to have it done.
Ça fait nounoune un peu. **–** That looks a bit silly.
Ça fait dur, ta situation. –Your situation seems pretty rough/pretty stupid.

Faisable : *adj.* – possible, do–able.

   🌿 *être faisable* – to be doable.

(Ça) Fait que… : *expr.* – so, that's why.

Il était fatigué, fait qu'on est rentré plus tôt. – He was tired, so we went home early.

Fait(e) : *adj.* – 1. done, complete. 2. done in, in trouble.

   🌿 *fait à l'os* – completely finished, completely done. *Lit.* done to the bone.
     Il est fait, là. – He's really in trouble now.

Faker : *v.t.* – to fake, to pretend.

Falle : *n.f.* – throat.

   🌿 *avoir la falle basse* - to have a long face, to be down.

Fantasmer : *v.i.* – to dream (of something).

Faque : *expr.* – *contr.* fait que (so, that's why).

Farce : *n.f.* – joke.

Fardouches : *n.f .Pl.*- underbrush, undergrowth.

Fauché : *adj.* – *sl.* broke, out of money.

Fendant(e) : *n.m. /fem. & adj.* – pretentious, arrogant (person).

Fermer : *v.t., v.i.* – *Fr.* to close, to shut.

> ❧ *fermer (un endroit)* – to close (a place, such as a bar).
> *Il est déjà 2 h 45, on va fermer la place !* – It's already 2:45am, we're going to close the place!
> ❧ *ferme ta soue !* – shut your mouth! *Lit.* Shut your sty.

Fesse : *n.f.* – *sl.* butt, rear–end, hind–quarters.

> ❧ *jouer au fesses*★ – to screw, to have sex with (someone).

Fesser : *v.i.* – 1. to strike, to hit head-first. 2. to have a kick, to be strong. Often used to describe a beverage, etc.

> *Lui, il a fessé dans le mur.* – He bashed (head–first) into the wall.
> *Aye, ça fesse, ta boisson !* – Hey, your drink really has a kick!
> ❧ *fesser dans le dash*- to be surprising, to be unexpected.

Fête : *n.f.* – 1. *Fr.* party. 2. birthday.

Fête de la Reine : *n.f.* – (Queen) Victoria day.

Fête du Travail : *n.f* – Labor day.

Fève : *n.f.* – *Fr.* bean.

> ❧ *fèves au lard* – baked beans.

Feu : *n.m.* – *Fr.* fire.

> ❧ *avoir le feu au cul*★ – to be furious. *Lit.* to have fire in the ass.
> ❧ *avoir le feu au passage*★ – to be furious. *Lit.* to have fire in the passage.

Fier-pet : *adj. & n.m./fem.* – proud, vain.

Fif, Fifi : *n.m. & adj.* – 1. homosexual (in attitude or action). Only used in the masculine. 2. *sl.* fraidy-cat, chicken.

Filer : *adj.* – to feel (well).

Non, je file pas bien, là. – No, I don't feel very well right now.

Filière : *n.f.* – filing cabinet.

Film de cul : *expr.* – porno film.

Fin(e) : *adj.* – sweet, likeable, gentle, nice, generous.

Il est tellement fin, ce gars-là! – He's such a great guy!

Fin : *n.f.* – Fr. end.

⚜ *fin de semaine* – weekend.
⚜ *fin de soirée* – (rest of) the evening.
   Bonne fin de soirée! – Have a good evening!

Finissant(e) : *n.m/f.* – graduating student.

Fitter : *v.t.* – to fit, to go (together).

Tout ça ne pourrait jamais fitter ensemble. – All that could never go together.
⚜ *faire fitter* – to adjust.
   Attends, je vais le faire fitter un peu mieux. – Hold on, I'm going to adjust it a bit further.

Flagger : *v.t.* - to hail, to flag (down).

⚜ *flagger un taxi* – to hail a cab.

Flagosse : *n.f.* – small problem or issue.

Flagosser : *v.i.* – to waste time, to do unimportant things.

Flanc-mou : *adj. & n.m./fem.* – lazy (person).

Flancher : *v.i.* – *Fr.* to fail, to go out of service.

Flash : *n.m..* – idea, thought.

Je viens d'avoir un flash. – I just had a thought.

Flasher : *v.i.* – to occur to (someone).

Juste après, l'idée m'a flashé. – Just afterwards, the idea occurred to me.

Flot : *n.m.*/fem. – child.

Oui, on a des flos à la maison. – Yes, we have kids at home.

Flopper : *v.i.* – to fail, to flop.

Flusher : *v.t.* – to purge, to flush, to dump.

Ils sortent plus ensemble, elle l'a flushé il y a trois jours. – They're not going out any more – she dumped him three days ago.

Flux : *n.m* – diarrhea.

Flyé : *adj.* – extravagant, extreme, *sl.* fly. Generally used to describe a person.

Focusser (sur) : *v.i.* – to focus (on).

Foirer : *v.i.* – 1. to party, to have fun. 2. *sl.* to tank, to fail.

Ça va foirer complètement après – That's going to completely tank afterwards.

Folie furieuse : *n.f.*/*expr* – mad panic.

C'était la folie furieuse au bureau pour le quart d'heure avant son arrivé – It was a mad panic in the office for the fifteen minutes before he arrived.

Forçant(e) : *adj.* – difficult, requiring force.

Formule-1 : *adj. & n.m.* – the best, top-notch. Reference to the annual Formula-1 race held in Montréal.

Fort(e) : *adj.* – *Fr.* strong.

   ❧ *boire du fort* – to drink alcohol. *Lit.* to drink some strong (stuff).

Fortiller : *v.i.* – to move non–stop, to twitch.

Fou : *adj.* – *Fr.* crazy, insane.

   ❧ *fou bracque* – completely nuts.
   ❧ *fou raide* – completely nuts.

Foufounes★ : *n.f.* – *sl.* butt, backside, rear–end.

   ❧ *(se) faire taper les foufounes* – to get a spanking.

Fouille : *n.m.* – fall, spill.

   ❧ *prendre une fouille* – to take a fall.

Fouler : *v.i.* – to shrink, to pull back.

Fournaise : *n.m.* – furnace, heating system.

Fourneau : *n.m.* – oven.

Fourrant : *adj.* – confusing, annoying, inconvenient, bad.

Fourré : *adj.* – confused, screwed-up.

(se) Fourrer★★★ : *v.t., v.i.* – 1. *sl.* to screw up, to err. 2. *sl.* to screw (sexual sense).

   ❧ *fourrer le chien* – to mess things up. *Lit.* to screw the dog.
     Je me suis fourré avec cette affaire-là. – I screwed myself with that deal.

Franchement ! : *expr.* – really!

Frapper : *v.t., v.i.* – *Fr.* to hit, to strike.

> ❧ *frapper dans le beurre* – to blow it, to miss one's chance.
> ❧ *frapper un nœud* - to hit a wall, to encounter a significant obstacle.

Freaker : *v.i.* – *sl.* to freak (out), to panic.

> *L'affaire m'a fait freaker pendant au moins une semaine.* – The whole deal freaked me out for at least a week.

Frencher : *v.t., v.i.* – to tongue/french kiss.

Frette : *adj.* – cold. (*Def.* froid*)*.

Frigidaire : *n.m.* – refrigerator.

Friler : *v.i.* – to shiver, to tremble (with cold, etc.)

Frileux(-euse) : *adj.* – quick to be cold. Generally said of a person.

> *Ma blonde est vraiment frileuse* – My girlfriend gets cold really quickly.

Fripé : *adj.* – wiped out, *sl.* wasted.

> *À cause du party, j'étais tout fripé le lendemain* – Because of the party, I was pretty wiped out the next morning.

Friper : *v.i.* – to waste.

Friperie : *n.f.* – second-hand (clothing) store.

Froque : *n.f.* – coat.

Frosté : *adj. – sl.* stoned, *sl.* wiped out, *sl.* out of it.

Après avoir passé toute la nuit au travail, j'étais pas mal frosté. – After spending all night at work, I was pretty zoned out.

Fru : *adj.* – frustrated. (*Contr.* frustré).

Frustré : *adj. – Fr.* upset, frustrated, annoyed.

Frustrer : *v.i. – Fr.* to upset, to frustrate, to annoy.

Ça me frustre un peu de ne pas pouvoir y aller. – It frustrates me a bit not to be able to go.

Fuck Friend★ : *n.m.* – lover, casual sex partner.

Fuck off!★★ : *expr.* – "Screw it!", "The hell with it, then!". Not generally a comment directed at a person, but instead the dismissal of a situation or intent.

Il y a trop de monde; fuck off, on reviendra demain. – There're too many people – screw it, let's come back tomorrow.

Fucké★★ : *adj. – sl.* screwed up, *sl.* fucked up. A less vulgar and visceral sense than in English.

- *fucké au boutte* – completely screwed up.
- *fucké ben raide★★* – completely screwed up. *Lit.* screwed good and stiff.
- *fucké dans la tête* – screwed up in the head, messed up.
  La situation est fuckée au boutte. – The situation is completely screwed up.

Fucker★★ : *v.t. – sl.* to screw up, *sl.* to fuck up.

- *fucker le chien* - 1. to screw around 2. to have difficulty doing something.

Full : *adj., adv.* – completely, very, fully.

Moi, j'ai full d'affaires à faire – I have lots of work to do.
Maman, le frigo est full vide ! – Mom, the fridge is completely empty!
❧ *à full pine* - at full speed.

Fun : *n.m.* – fun, enjoyment.

Hé ! c'est le fun, ça ! – Hey, that's cool!
❧ *avoir du fun* – to have fun, to have a good time.
    On va avoir du fun demain. – We're going to have a good time tomorrow.
❧ *(un) fun noir*– a crazy good time.
❧ *pour le fun* – for the fun of it, not serious.
    Je ne voulais pas vraiment leur deranger – c'était juste pour le fun – I didn't really mean to bother them – it was just for the fun of it.

Funerailles : *n.f. pl.* - funeral

G

Galerie : *n.f.*– balcony, terrace.

Galette : *n.f.* – *Fr.* biscuit, shortbread.

❧ *faire la galette* – to make (a lot of) money.

Galon : *n.m.* – measuring tape.

Galvaude : *n.f.* – poutine (french fries and lumps of cheese covered in gravy) mixed with chicken and peas.

Galvauder : *v.i.* – 1. to tease, to flirt, to pursue the opposite sex. 2. to botch a job.

Galvaudeux(-euse) : *n.m./fem.* – one who gallantly pursues opposite sex.

Game : *adj* – willing, prepared

> ❧ *Être game* – to be game, to be willing

Garde ! : *expr.* – look! (imperative, *Contr.* regarder*)*.

> ❧ *Garde donc !* – Look at that!
> *Garde, je n'ai plus le temps pour ça.* – Look, I don't have time for this anymore.

Garde-robe : *n.m.* – closet, wardrobe.

Gardon : *expr.* – "Look, then". *Def.* regarde, donc.

> *Gardon, il faut que je te parles !* – Look, I gotta talk with you.
> ❧ *Gardon ça !* – Check that out!

Garderie : *n.f.* – *Fr.* daycare center.

Gardien(ne) : *n.masc./fem.* – *Fr. babysitter.*

Garnotte : *n.f.* – pebble. *N.f. pl :* Gravel.

Garnotter : *v.t.* – to whip something (at something/someone), to throw something.

Garrocher : *v.t.* – 1. to toss, throw, or project something. 2. to work quickly or carelessly.

> *Les enfants garrochaient des roches au chien.* – The children threw rocks at the dog.

Gars : *n.m.* – *Fr.* guy. Used in the possessive (*mon gars*) to add emphasis when speaking with someone, in somewhat the same sense as *sl.* "dude" or *sl.* "man" in English.

Là, mon gars, j'étais complètement crevé. – At that point, dude, I was totally exhausted.

Gâté : *adj.* – spoiled

Gâter : *v.i.* – to spoil (someone).

Gaz : *n.m.* – *Fr.* gas, fuel.

Gazer : *v.t.* – to fill up (with gas).

Gelé : *adj.* – 1. *Fr.* frozen. 2. *sl.* stoned, *sl.* baked (from drugs).

Geler : *v.i.* – to be freezing, to be cold.

Moi, je gele, là. – Well, I'm freezing.

Gênant(e) : *adj.* – *Fr.* intimidating, blocking, causing hesitation.

Je trouvais son attitude un peu gênante. – I found his attitude somewhat intimidating.

Gêné : *adj.* – shy, hesitant, nervous.

Je suis gêné de parler à mon patron à ce sujet. – I'm hesitant to talk with my boss about that.

Genre : *n.m., expr.* – 1. *Fr.* kind of, type. 2. *sl.* like. The latter usage is almost identical to the slang American use of the word *like* in casual speech.

C'est le genre de gars qui ferait ça. – He's the kind of guy who'd do that.
C'est est un gars cool, genre. – He's, like, a cool guy.

Gérant(e) : *n.m/f.* – manager.

Gigoter : *v.i.* – to hurry up, to move quickly.

Gilet : *n.m.* – light shirt (especially a sports shirt).

Gîte (touristique) : *n.m.* – Bed & Breakfast (B&B).

Gizmut : *n.m.* – *sl.* gizmo.

Glace : *n.f.* – ice cube.

Glandouneux(euse) : *adj. & n.m./fem .* – lazy oaf, do-nothing, slacker.

Gnochon(ne) : *adj. .& n.m./f.* – ignoramus, uneducated (person).

Goaler : *v.i.* – 1. to act as a goalie (soccer). 2. to work very hard.

Goaleur : *n.m.* – goalie.

Gossage : *n.m.* – fooling around, a waste of time.

Gogosse : *n.f.* – small (cheap or unimportant) object.

Gomme : *n.f.* – 1. *Fr.* pencil eraser. 2. chewing gum.

Gosser : *v.i.* – 1. to fiddle with, to fool with (something) 2. to waste time on the details. 3. to bug, to bother.

Gosses★ : *n.f.* – 1. *Fr.* children. 2. testicles.

  ❄ *avoir des gosses★* – *sl.* to have balls, to be brave.
  ❄ *partir sur une gosse★* - to leave (somewhere) quickly.

Gosseux(euse) : *adj. & n.m./fem.* – *sl.* a big talker, one who thinks him/herself bigger than their breeches.

Gougounes : *n.f.* – beach sandals.

Goût : *n.m.* – *Fr.* taste.

> *avoir le goût (de faire quelque chose)* – to feel like (doing something).
> *J'ai le goût de faire l'amour.* – I feel like making love.

Grafigne : *n.f.* – scratch.

Grafigner : *v.t.* – 1. to scratch, to graze. 2. to mar, to damage.

Il s'est fait grafigner par son frère. – He was scratched by his brother.
S'il continue de même, ça va grafigner ma réputation. – If he continues this way, it will hurt my reputation.

Grand monde : *expr.* – high society, the upper crust.

Graine** : *n.f.* – 1. schlong, penis. 2. Idiot, fool.

Grano : *n.m.* – contr. *Granola*

Granola : *n.m.* – health food fanatic.

Gras dur : *expr.* - lucky. *Lit.* hard fat.

Grassette : *adj.* – chubby, overweight (used for a girl or woman)

Son visage est belle, mais est toutefouis un peu grassette – She's visually pretty, but a little chunky even so.

Grassouillette : adj – chubby, overweight (used for a girl or woman)

Gratin : *n.m.* – the who's-who, the upper crust.

Le gratin artistique est venu cette soirée là. – The who's-who of the art world came that evening.

Gratte : *n.f.* – 1. snowplow. 2. hand-held ice scraper.

T'es malchanceux, mon homme, la gratte a déja passé. – You're out of luck, my friend, the snowplow already went by.

Gratte-la-cenne : *n.m.* – miser. *Lit.* cent-scraper.

Gratter : *v.i.* – to be stingey, to be tight-fisted.

Gratteux(-euse) : *n.m./f. & adj.* – (one who is)avaricious; stingy or tight-fisted.

Gratteux : *n.m.* – (scratchable) lottery, ticket.

Gravel : *n.f.* – gravel.

Gréluche : *n.f.* – low-class or unintelligent woman.

Gripette : *adj.* Crabby, Cranky.

T'es pas mal gripette avant ton café le matin ! - You're pretty cranky before your coffee in the morning !

Gruau : *n.m.* – oatmeal, hot cereal.

Gréyé : *adj.* – prepared, equipped, ready.

   être bien gréyé – to be all set, to be ready.

(se) Gréyer : *v.i.* – to prepare, to equip oneself.

Griller : *v.t.* – to tan, to bake in the sun.

Grippe : *n.f.* – *Fr.* the flu.

Grippé : *adj.* – *Fr.* infected with the flu.

Grosse Mol : *expr.* – a large Molson beer.

(se) Grouiller : *v.i.* – to hurry up, to move quickly.

Guenille : *n.f.* - 1. rag. 2. *n.f.pl :* (cheap) clothes.

> *À chaque guenille son torchon* – To every girl her guy. *Lit.* to each cloth its rag.

Gueule★ : *n.f.* – *Fr.* maw, mouth (of an animal). Slang reference to one's mouth, or the words which come from it.

> *avoir la gueule fendue jusqu'aux oreilles.* – to be grinning from ear to ear.

Gugus : *n.m.* – small (cheap or unimportant) object.

Guidoune★★ : *n.f.* – whore, slut.

H

Habit : *n.m.* – suit of clothes.

> *Je lui ai acheté un bel habit pour Noël.* – I bought him a nice suit of clothes for Christmas.

Hab : *n.m.* – *contr.* habitant.

Habiller : *v.t.* – to dress.

> *être habillé comme lachienne à Jacques* – to be badly dressed. *Lit.* to be dressed like Jacques' dog.

Habitant(e)★ : *adj & n.m. /f.* – redneck, country bumpkin.

Hambourgeois : *n.m.* – hamburger.

Haut : *adj.* – *Fr.* high.

  🌿 *en haut de* – above.

Hein? : *expr.* – What?

Herbe à puce : *n.f.* – poison ivy.

Heure : *n.f.* – *Fr.* hour.

  🌿 *heures d'affaires* – business hours.

Hèvé : *adj.* – difficult, serious. *Eng.* heavy.

La situation de sa mère est assez hèvé. – Her mother's situation is pretty serious.

Historique : *n.f.* – story, tale.

C'est une historique assez intéressante. – It's a pretty interesting story.

Hiver : *n.m.* – *Fr.* winter.

  🌿 *Qu'est-ce que ça mange en hiver?* – What is (it) like? *Lit.* What does it eat in wintertime?

Homme : *n. masc* – *Fr.* man. Often used in the possessive (*mon homme*), to add emphasis when speaking with someone, in somewhat the same sense as *sl.* "dude" or *sl.* "man" in English.

Là, mon homme, j'étais complètement crevé. – At that point, dude, I was totally exhausted.

Hostic★ : *expl.* – see *ostic*.

Hostie★★ : *expl.* – see *ostie*.

Horaire : *n.m.* – schedule, timetable.

Veux-tu me vérifier l'horaire ? – Would you check the schedule for me?

Hot : *adj.* – high-quality, neat, *sl.* hot.

Il est hot, ton char ! – Your car is really hot!

Huard : *n.m.* – dollar.

I

Ici : *adv.* – *Fr.* here, in this place.

❄ *D'ici…* - Between now and…
   D'ici un an, il sera fait. – Within a year, it will be done..

Icitte : *adv.* – here. *Déf.* ici.

Il n'y a pas de trouble ! : *expr.* - No problem!

Incontournable : *adj.* – unforseeable, unavoidable.

Inécoutable : *adj.* – unlistenable.

Intéressant(e) : *adj.* – 1. *Fr.* (intellectually) interesting, stimulating. 2. important, a good thing. *N.B.* International French and English only use the former of these two meanings.

C'est une histoire intéressante ! – That's an interesting story!
Paul ne vient pas, donc ça serait intéressant que tu viennes avec nous. – Paul isn't coming, so it would be a good thing if you came with us.

Intraduisible : *adj.* – unable to be translated.

Introduire : *v.i.* – *Fr.* to introduce, present. Québécois often use this word (rather than *présenter*) for personal introductions.

Instant (à l') : *n.m.* – now, at the moment.

> *Il n'est pas parlable à l'instant.* – He's not able to be talked with at the moment.
> *Il faut que tu le fasses à l'instant où je te le dis.* – You need to do it right when I tell you.

Itou : *conj.* – also.

J

Jack : *n.m.* – Jack.

> ❧ *bon Jack* – a good guy.
> ❧ *grand Jack* - a big guy.

Jacker : *v.t.* – to jack up, to elevate.

Jambon : *n.m.* – *Fr.* ham, hamhock.

> ❧ *(Un) gros jambon* – a self-satisfied individual

Jammé : *adj.* – stuck, jammed.

Jammer : *v.t.* – 1. to jam, to force. 2. *sl.* to jam, to play music improvisationally.

Jaquette : *n.f.* – nightshirt.

Jarnigoine : *n.m/f.* – 1. chatterbox, talkative person. 2. Intelligence, initiative

> ❧ *avoir le jarnigoine* – to be intelligent.

Jaser : *v.i.* – to chat with, to speak with (someone).

Ouais, on a jasé hier. – Yeah, we spoke yesterday.

Jasette : *n.f.* – chat, quick conversation.

❧ *piquer une jasette* – to have a chat.

Jaspiner : *v.i.* – to complain constantly, to lament.

Jaspineux(euse) : *adj & n.m./fem.* – one who complains constantly.

Jériboire!★ : *expr.* – Heck!, Darn it!

Jésus-Christ!★ : *expl.* – Jesus Christ!

Job : *n.f.* – job, work.

❧ *job de bras* – *sl.* gruntwork, labor. *Lit.* arm-work.

Jos★★ : *masc. pl.* – breasts.

Joual : *n.m.* – popular language, slang.

Joualvert★ : *expr.* – Hell!

❧ *être en (beau) joualvert★* – to be furious.

Jouer : *v.t., v.i.* – Fr. to play.

❧ *jouer au fesses★* – to screw, to have sex with (someone).
❧ *jouer aux quilles* – to bowl, to go bowling.

Joues : *n.m. pl.* – affectionate term for a woman's behind. *Lit.* cheeks.

Jus : *n.m.* – 1. *Fr.* juice. 2. *Fr.* sauce, stew. 3. electricity, current.

❧ *être dans le jus* – *sl.* to be swamped, to be busy. *Lit.* to be in the sauce.

Juste : *adj.* − 1. *Fr.* just, right (ethical sense). 2. close to, on the verge of something.

> *C'est juste un peu trop petit.* − It's just a little too small.
> *C'était juste!* − He just made it!
> ❧ *au juste* − actually.

K

Kaline : *expl.* − *sim.* Dammit! (gentler form of câlisse).

Kessé ça? : *expr.* − What is that? (*Contr. Qu'est-ce que c'est, ça*)

Kétaine : *adj.* − taseless, bad.

> ❧ *Kétaine au boutte.* − completely tasteless.
> *Ses vêtements sont kétaines au boutte.* − His clothes are completely tasteless

Kick : *n.m.* − kick, blow.

> ❧ *avoir un kick sur (quelqu'un)* − to have a crush on (someone).

Kicker : *v.t.* − 1. to kick, propel forward. 2. to complain.

Kioute : *adj.* − cute.

Kodak : *n.m.* − camera.

Kossé? : *expr.* − What is it? *Def.* Qu'est-ce que c'est?

L

Là : *expr.* – 1. *Fr.* there, in that place. 2. now.

> ✄ *Là, là…* – Now about that…

Là-dessus : *conj.* – about it, about that.

> *Je voudrais bien te parler là–dessus.* – I'd like to talk with you about that.
> *Je vais mettre un homme là-dessus.* – I'll put a man on it.

Lâche : *adj* – *Fr.* lazy, laxidasical.

> ✄ *lâche comme un âne.* – lazy as an ass (donkey).

Lâcher : *v.t., v.i.* – 1. to quit, to give up, to let go. 2. to lick. 3. to fail, to give out.

> *Mon cellulaire va lacher bientôt* – My cellphone is going to give out pretty soon.
> ✄ *lâcher un coup de fil* – to give someone a phone call.
> ✄ *lâcher une fiouse* – to fart, to pass wind. *Lit.* To pop a fuse.
> ✄ *lâcher son fou* – to let one's hair down, to let loose.
> ✄ (se) *lâcher lousse* – to let one's self loose (to have fun, etc)
> ✄ *Lâche pas la patate !* – Don't give up! *Lit.* Don't let go of the potato.
> ✄ *lâcher un pet* – to fart, to pass wind.
> ✄ *lâcher un wack* – to let out a yell.

Lambineux (-euse) : *n.m./fem. & adj.* – one who is indecisive or hesitant.

Langue : *n.f.* – 1. *Fr.* tongue. 2. *Fr.* language, spoken tongue.

> ✄ *avoir la langue à terre* – 1. to be exhausted. 2. to be very hungry. *Lit.* to have (one's) tongue on the ground.
> ✄ *avoir la langue sale* – to have a dirty mouth. *Lit.* to have a dirty tongue.
> ✄ *sur le bout de la langue* – on the tip of (one's) tongue.

Lavage : *n.m.* – laundry.

J'ai tellement de lavage à faire ! – I have so much laundry to do!

Lave-auto : *n.m.* – carwash.

Laveuse : *n.f.* – washing machine.

Légume : *n.m.* – *Fr.* vegetable.

   ❧ *la grosse légume* – the big cheese (the important person).
   Lit. big vegetable.

Lendemain de veille : *n.m. expr.* – the "morning after" (a party, etc).

Levée de fonds : *n.m./expr.* – fundraising.

Lever : *v.i/v.t* - 1. *Fr.* to lift, to raise. 2. to get out of bed.

   ❧ *se lever le coude* – to have several beers. *Lit.* to lift one's elbow.
   ❧ *se lever le gros orteil au nord* - to get up on the wrong side of the bed, to be cranky. *Lit.* to get up with one's big toe pointed north
   ❧ *se lever du pied gauche* – to get up on the wrong side of the bed, to be cranky. *Lit.* to get up on the left foot.

Lettres carrées : *n.m pl..* – capital letters. *Lit.* square letters.

Libre-service : *n.m.* – self-service.

Licencié : *adj.* – license-holder, generally of a liquor license. Restaurants in Québec often display the sign *"Licence complete"* to indicate they sell alcohol.

Lichette : *n.f.* - hickey, red mark left on the skin from a kiss.

Licheux (-euse) : *adj & n.m/f.* – ass-kisser, brown-noser.

Lift : *n.m.* – ride, lift (in a vehicle).

✺ *donner un lift* – to give (someone) a lift.

✺ *quêteux de lift* – one who incessently seeks out free rides.

Ligne : *n.f.* – 1. *Fr.* waiting line. 2. phone line.

✺ *en bout de ligne* – ultimately, finally *(Lit.* at the end of the line).

Limonade : *n.f.* – Lemonade.

Linge : *n.m.* – clothes, or most anything made from material (underwear, sheets, napkins, etc).

Elle a mis tout son linge dans un sac vert. – She put all his clothes in a garbage bag.

Liqueur : *n.f.* – *Fr.* after-dinner drink.

✺ *liqueur douce* – soda, carbonated non–alcoholic drink.

Liseux(euse) : *n.m./fem. & adj.* – bookworm, one who reads constantly.

Loadé(e) : *adj.* – 1. loaded (filled). 2. loaded (with money).

Le gars à qui appartient ce char-là, il est pas mal loadé. – The guy who owns that car is pretty loaded.

Loader : *v.t.* – to load, to fill up.

Logis : *n.m.* – *Fr.* apartment, house, place of residence.

Lotion après-rasage : *n.m.* – after-shave lotion.

Lousse : *adj.& n.m.* – 1. loose, slack, play. 2. generous (in a monetary sense).

Lui, il a toujours été un peu lousse avec son argent. – He's always been pretty generous with his money.

✺ *(se) lâcher lousse* – to let one's self loose (to have fun, etc).

Lumière : *n.f.* – 1. *Fr.* light. 2. cars' headlights. 3. traffic light.

Mets tes lumières ! – Put your lights on!
Regarde, la lumière va changer. – Look, the light's going to change.

Luncher : *v.i.* – to have lunch.

Lutter : *v.t.* – to hit (with a car).

J'ai lutté mon char trois jours après l'avoir achété – I crashed my car three days after I bought it.

M

Mâchable : *adj.* – chewable.

(se) Maigner (de cul**) : to hurry up, to move one's ass.

Mal pris : *expr.* – in trouble, in bad shape.

Magané : *adj.* – 1. ruined, battered, wrecked. 2. exhausted.

Je pense que le fauteuil est un peu trop magané pour garder. – I think the couch is a bit too far gone to keep.
J'ai travaillé jusqu'à trois heures du matin, alors là je suis complètement magané. – I was at work 'til three in the morning, so now I'm completely wrecked.

Maganer : *v.t.* – 1. to damage, to cause harm to. 2. to treat something/someone badly.

Je ne veux pas maganer mon veston. – I don't want to damage my suit jacket.

Magasinage : *n.m.* – shopping.

Magasiner : *v.i.* – to go shopping.

Main : *n.f.* – *Fr.* hand.

    avoir les mains pleines de pouces – to be all thumbs.

(la) Main : *n.f.* – *sl.* main drag, main road in a town.

    On s'est promenés sur la main pendant trois heures. – We walked along the main drag for three hours.

Malin(e) : *adj.* – 1. angry 2. nasty, aggressive.

Malle : *n.f.* – mail. *Def. Engl.* mail.

    aller à malle – to go get the mail.

Maller : *v.t.*- to mail, to send.

Manche : *n.f.* – handle.

    branler dans le manche – to hesitate when making a decision. *Lit.* to hesitate in the handle.

Manquer : *v.t., v.i.* – *Fr.* to miss.

    manquer le bateau – to miss the boat (figuratively or literally).

Manger : *v.t.* – to eat.

    se faire manger – *sl.* to get chewed out.
    manger (ses) bâs – 1. to be uncomfortable with one's speech or action, *sim.* "open mouth, extract foot". 2. to worry or panic. *Lit.* to eat one's socks.
    se laisser manger la laine sur le dos – to lose one's shirt, to be exploited. *Lit.* to let the wool be eaten from your back.
    mange de la marde★★! – eat shit!
    mange de la schnoute★ – eat shit!

❄ *en manger une* − *sl.* to 'get it', to get in trouble, to be reprimanded. *Lit.* to eat one.

❄ *Qu'est-ce que ça mange en hiver?* − What is (it) like? *Lit.* What does it eat in wintertime?

Marche : *n.f.* − *Fr.* a stroll, a walk.

❄ *prendre une marche* − to take a walk.
   On va aller prendre une marche jusqu'à midi. − We're going to go for a walk until noon.

Marcher : v.i. − 1. *Fr.* to work, to function properly. 2. *Fr.* to walk.

❄ *marcher à mort* − to work beautifully. *Lit.* to work to death.
❄ *marcher à planche* − to work perfectly. *Lit.* to work flat-out.

Marde★★ : *n.f., expr.* − shit. (*Déf. merde*).

❄ *plein de marde★★* − full of shit.
❄ *mouche à marde★* - clinger, annoying individual whose presence can't be escaped. *Lit.* shit-fly.
❄ *tache à marde★* - clinger, annoying individual whose presence can't be escaped. *Lit.* shit-stain.

Mardeux : *adj.* & *n.m. /f.* − lucky, fortunate (person).

(se) Marier : *v.t.* − to marry.

Maringouin : *n.m.* mosquito.

Marmaille : *n.f.* − children, kids.

(en) Masse : *n.f.* − 1. a lot of, much of. 2. enough, plenty.

Ça glisse en masse ! − It's really slippery
On en a en masse, merci. − We have plenty, thanks.

Matcher : *v.t.* – to put together, to match.

Matrone : *n.f.* – 1. mother-in-law. 2. matron, head of a household.

Mauditement bon : *expr.* – Wickedly good.

Mautadit : *expl.* – Damn! Softer form of *maudit* (*Fr.* cursed, damned).

Méchant : *adj. & adv.* – 1. *Fr.* wicked, mean, nasty. 2. very, really.

Lui, c'est un gars assez méchant. – He's a pretty mean guy.
Ça va être méchant dur. – That's going to be really hard.

Mèche : *n.f.* – 1. *Fr.* fuse, wick. 2. hair highlights, colored strands.

avoir la mèche courte – to have a short fuse, to be quick-tempered.
Je vais ajouter des mèches bleues demain. – I'm going to add some blue highlights to my hair tomorrow.

Médaille : *n.f.* – coin.

deux côtés de la médaille – *Lit.* both sides of the coin.

(la) Meilleur des mondes : *expr.* – an ideal world.

Mêlant : *adj.* – *Fr.* confusing, disorienting.

C'était mêlant un peu de voir les deux ensemble. – It was a bit confusing to see the two of them together.

Mêlé : *adj.* – *Fr.* confused, mixed up.

(de) Même : *adv.* – like this/that.

Je n'aime pas les gars de même. – I don't like guys like that.

Même à ça : *expr.* – even so.

Mémérage : *n.f.* – gossip, chit-chat.

Mémère : *n.m./fem. & adj.* – talkative, loquacious (person).

Mémérer : *v.i.* – to gossip, to chatter.

Méné : *n.m.* – 1. minnow. 2. person with little weight or influence in a given situation.

> *Même s'il est là depuis cinq ans, il est toujours un méné au bureau.*- Although he's been there for five years, he still has no influence the office.

Mener : *v.t.* – *Fr.* to lead, to conduct.

> *mener le diable* – to make a racket, cause a disturbance. *Lit.* to lead the devil.

Menterie : *n.f.* – lie, untruth.

Mettre : *v.t.* – 1. *Fr.* to put/place. 2. (se faire) mettre★★★ to get laid, to have sex with someone.

> *Mets ça dans ta pipe puis fume !* – Put that in your pipe and smoke it!
> *Il sortait ce soir juste pour essayer de se mettre★★★.* – He went out tonight just to try and get laid.
> *mettre la musique dans le piton*- to play music at high volume.

Mets-en ! : *expr.* – "That's for sure!" *sl.* "Totally"! *Lit.* Add some more.

Minoucher : *v.i.*– to caress, to kiss, to cuddle with (someone).

Minoucher : *v.t.* – to flatter (someone), to butter (someone) up.

Minoune : *n.f.* – 1. old car. 2. cat, kitten. Also used as an affectionate word for a young girl.

> *Oui, ma minoune ?* – Yes, my darling?

Misère : *n.f.* – difficulty.

- *avoir de la misère* – to have difficulty.

Mitaine : *n.f.* – glove, mitten.

- *faire à mitaine* – to do by hand. *Lit.* to do by mitten.

Moffer : *v.i.* – to mess up, to miss (something).

J'ai essayé lui faire du sushi, mais je l'ai completemment moffé. – I tried to make him sushi, but I completely messed it up.

Moine★★ : *n.m.* – 1. *Fr.* monk. 2. *sl.* dick, penis.

Molle : *n.f* – soft ice cream.

Mollo : *adj.* – chilled-out, relaxed.

Monde : *n.m.* – 1. *Fr.* world. 2. *Fr.* people in the world.

- *(du) ben bon monde* - friendly folk, good people.
- *comme du monde* – the "correct way" to do something. *Lit.* "as other folks"

Mononcle : *adj.* – old-style, old-fashioned.

- *faire mononcle* – to be old-fashioned, to seem old-fashioned.
  Je ne veux pas amener le tapis avec moi, ça fait trop mononcle. – I don't want to bring the carpet, it's too old-fashioned.
  Ouais, ça fait un peu mononcle, mais ce n'est pas grave. – Yeah, it's a bit old-style, but that's not a problem.

Monter : *v.i., v.t.* – *Fr.* to go up, to rise.

- *monter d'une coche* – to go up a notch, to improve.

Mordée : *n.f.* – bite.

C'est sûr qu'il a pris une mordée dans ton profit. – It's certain that he took a bite out of your profit.

Mort : *n.f.* – *Fr.* death.

- *à mort* – a lot, completely.
- *Son chien est mort* – (*expr*) to be done-in, to be finished. *Lit.* His dog is dead.

Motoneige : *n.f.* – *Fr.* snowmobile.

Moton : *n.m.* – *Fr.* bump, knot, lump.

- *avoir le moton (dans le gorge)* – 1. to be choked up, to have a lump in one's throat. 2. to be wealthy.
  Quand elle lui a dit qu'elle l'aimait, ça se voyait qu'il avait le moton.
  – When she told him she loved him, you could see how choked up he was.

Mouche : *n.f.* – *Fr.* fly.

- *mouche à cheval* – horsefly.
- *mouche à chevreuil*- deerfly.
- *mouche à feu*- lightning bug.
- *mouche à marde★* - clinger, annoying individual whose presence can't be escaped. *Lit.* shit-fly.

Moufette : *n.m.* – skunk.

Mouillasser : *v.i.* – to drizzle, to sprinkle (light rain).

Mouillassseux : *adj.* – rainy, drizzly.

Mouiller : *v.i.* – 1. *Fr.* to wet. 2. to be rainy, to be wet.

Il va mouiller toute la fin de semaine. – It's going to rain the whole weekend.

Moumoune : *adj.* & *n.m./fem.* – 1. wimp, wuss, fraidy-cat. 2. homosexual.

Moumoute : *n.f.* – hairpiece.

Mourant(e) : *adj.* – hysterical, hilarious.

J'ai vu ce film-là, c'était mourant ! – I saw that film, it was a riot!

Mouton : *n.m.* – *Fr.* sheep.

❧ *revenir à (ses) moutons* – to come back to the subject at hand. *Lit.* to get back to (one's) sheep.

Mouve : *n.m.* – move (allegorical or literal).

C'est un mouve que je ne peux vraiment pas expliquer. – That's a move I really can't explain.

Mouver : *v.i.* – to move (change residences).

Moyens : *n.m. pl.* – *Fr.* the means, the methods, the techniques.

Avez-vous un moyen de le faire livrer chez moi ? – Do you have a way to get it delivered to my place?
Il n'a pas les moyens financiers pour déménager à Westmount. – He doesn't have the financial means to move to Westmount.

Musique à bouche : *n.f.* – harmonica.

N

Nanane : *n.m.* - 1. candy. 2. treat, goodie.

> *Elle pleure parce qu'elle n'a pas eu son nanane* – She's crying because she didn't get her goodie.

Narc : *n.m.* – drug squad, narcotics law enforcement.

Necker : *v.i.* – *sl.* to make out, *sl.* to neck, to kiss.

Neiger : *v.i.* – *Fr.* to snow.

> ❄ *avoir vu neiger* – to have experience. *Lit.* to have seen it snow before.

Nerf : *n.m.* – *Fr.* nerve.

> ❄ *tomber sur les nerfs* – to annoy, to exasperate. *Lit.* to fall upon one's nerves.
> ❄ *Les nerfs !* – *sl.* Chill out! Calm down!

Net-fret-sec ! : *expr.* – cut and dry. *Lit.* clean-cold-dry.

Nettoyeur : *n.m.* – dry-cleaner.

(au) Neutre : *adj.* – (in) neutral gear (in a car).

Nez : *n.m.* – *Fr.* nose.

> ❄ *avoir le nez brun* – to be a brown-noser.

Niaisage : *n.m.* – fooling around, stupidity.

Niaiseux (-euse) : *n.m./fem., adj.* – idiot(ic), fool(ish).

> *T'es ben niaiseux !* – You're a real pain!

Niaiser : *v.i.* – 1. to tease, to annoy. 2. to string someone along, to waste someone's time.

✖ *Arrêt de niaiser pas avec la puck !* – Stop fooling around! *Lit.* stop fooling around with the puck.

NIP : *n.m.* – PIN code, password (for cash machine).

Nœud : *n.m.* – *Fr.* knot.

✖ *frapper un nœud* - to hit a wall, to encounter a significant obstacle.

Noirceur : *n.f.* – darkness, night.

Nombril du monde : *expr.* – egocentric person. *Lit.* bellybutton of the earth

✖ *(se) prendre pour le nombril du monde*- to believe one's self to be the most important thing. *Lit.* to take one's self as the bellybutton of the earth.

Nono : *adj. & n.m. /fem.* – idiot, *sl.* bozo.

Noune ★★★ : *n.f.* – reference to female genitalia.

Nounoune : *n. masc. /fem. & adj.* – idiot, imbecile.

Sois pas nounoune, toi ! – Don't be an idiot!

Nounours : *n.m.* – Teddy bear.

Nous-autres : *pron.* – we all, we.

Nouveau(x) : *adj. masc.* – *Fr.* new.

✖ *attendre du nouveau* – to be expecting a child; to be pregnant. *Lit.* to wait for a new (one).

O

Occasions : *n.f. pl.* – bargains.

Œuf : *n.m* – *Fr.* egg.

- *œufs (au) miroir* – eggs "over"
- *œufs brouillés* – scrambled eggs

Onguent : *n.m.* – medicinal cream.

- *(ne pas être) de l'onguent* – to not be expensive. *Lit.* to (not be) medicinal cream.
  Mets-en, c'est pas de l'onguent. – Go ahead (*impl.* add more), it's not that expensive.

O.P.C. – *expr.* – as quickly as possible. *Contr.* au plus crissant.

Opérer : *v.t.* – to make (something) function.

- *faire opérer* – to make (something) work.

Ordi(n) : *n.m.* – computer *(abbr. ordinateur).*

Oreilles de Christ : *n.f. pl.* – fried pig ears.

Orignal : *n.m.* – moose.

- *câler l'orignal* – to throw up, to puke. *Lit.* to call the moose.

Oreille : *n.f.* – *Fr.* ear.

- *oreilles de crisse* – fried salted pig fat. Traditional Québec dish served in a *cabane à sucre.*
- *avoir les oreilles dans le crin* – 1. to be careful, fearing something or someone. 2. to be in a bad mood. *Lit.* to have one's ears in horse-hair.

Orteil : *n.m. – Fr.* toe.

  🌟 *se lever le gros orteil au nord* – to get up on the wrong side of the bed, to be cranky. *Lit.* to get up with one's big toe pointed north

Ostic★ : *expl.* – softer form of *ostie*.

Ostie★★ : *expl. – equiv.* goddam! Derives from the French word for "Host", from the Catholic liturgy.

Ostination : *n.f.* – arguement, disagreement.

(s')Ostiner : *v* – to argue, to disagree.

  C'est sûr qu'il va m'ostiner là-dessus. – It's certain that he'll argue with me about it.

Ostineux(-euse) : *n.m/f & adj.*- argumentative person.

Ou : *prep. – Fr.* or, else.

  🌟 *oubedon* – or else (*contr.* ou bien donc).

Ouache ! : *excl.* – yuck!

Ouair : *v.t.* – to see (*Def.* voir).

  On va ouair un bon show ce soir. – We'll see a good show tonight.

Ouaouaron : *n.m.* – large frog.

Oubedon : *expr.* – otherwise, or else. *Def.* Ou bien donc.

Ousque : *expr.* – ou est-ce que (*Contr. Ou est-ce que*)

  Ousquilé ?- Where is he?

Oui allô ? : *expr. idiom.* – Hello? Used when responding to the telephone.

Oupéllaie ! : *expr.* – 1. "Whoa!" 2. "Oups!", "Whoops!"

Ours : *n.m.* – *Fr.* bear

 ❧ *(un) ours mal- lêché* – a scruffy person. *Lit.* a badly-licked bear.

P

Pain : *n.m.* – *Fr.* bread.

 ❧ *être né pour un petit pain* – born to be mediocre. *Lit.* to be born for little bread.

Pagette : *n.f.* – pager, beeper.

Pagosse : *n.f.* – thing, object.

Palettes : *n.f. pl.* – front teeth.

Palmarès : *n.m.* – hit list, Top 40.

Pancarte : *n.f.* – sign.

Panneau : *n.m.* – sign.

Pantoute : *expr.* – not at all, not entirely (*Def.* pas en toute).

 ❧ *Pas pire, pantoute !* – Not bad, not bad at all!

Papier sablé : *n.f.* – sandpaper.

Paquet : *n.m.* – a bunch of, a lot of.

 ❧ *paquet d'affaires* – a bunch of things.

Paqueté(e) : *adj.* – 1. loaded, drunk. 2. completely filled, packed. *Lit.* stuffed.

   (se) paqueter la gueule – to get drunk

   (se) paqueter la fraise – to get drunk.

(se) Paqueter : *v.i.* – to get loaded, to get drunk.

Pardessus : *n.m.* – 1. overcoat. 2. rubbers, boots.

Par exemple : *expr., prep.* – 1. actually. 2. *Fr.* for example. 3. however, though. The first definition is more common usage:

Je n'y suis pas allé, par exemple. – I didn't go, actually.
Moi, par exemple, je ne suis pas encore convaincu. – I, however, am not yet convinced.

Parcomètre : *n.m.* – parking meter.

Pareil(eille) : *adj.* – *Fr.* same.

   pareil comme… – the same as…

Parlable : *adj.* – communicative, able to be spoken with/to.

Il est fâché en ce moment, et donc pas très parlable. – He's mad right now, and so not very communicative.

Parler : *v.i.* – *Fr.* to talk, to speak.

   parler dans le dos – to talk behind someone's back.
   parler les baguettes en l'air – to gesticulate while talking

Parlure : *n.f.* – slang.

Partir : *v.i.* – 1. *Fr.* to leave. 2. to start.

On va bientôt partir. – We're going to leave soon.

Veux-tu partir le micro-ondes, s'il te plaît ? – Would you start the microwave, please?

❄ *partir en affaires* – to start a business.

❄ *partir pour la gloire* – 1. to head off on a mission. 2. to be pregnant. *Lit.* to head off to glory.

❄ *partir sur une gosse★* - to leave (somewhere) quickly.

❄ *partir sur une "go"* – to go on a bender, to go all out.

Pas d'affaire ! : *expr* – There's no question!

Pas d'allure : *n.m./f.* – gauche or maladroit person.

Passage : *n.m.* – corridor, hall.

Passe-Passe : *n.m.* – workaround, alternative method.

(se) Passer : *v.i.* – 1. *Fr.* to pass, pass off. 2. to give, to loan.

As-tu trois dollars à me passer ? – Could you loan me three bucks?

❄ *(se faire) passer (quelque chose) en dessous du nez* – miss a good occasion. *Lit.* to have (something) go right under your nose.

❄ *(se faire) passer un sapin* – to be had, to get a bad deal. *Lit.* to be handed a fir tree.

❄ *passer au cash* – to get what one deserves.

❄ *passer au dép(anneur)* – to swing by the convenience store.

❄ *passer tout droit* – to oversleep. *Lit. to go right through.*

❄ *passer au feu* – to burn down.

❄ *passer la nuit ur la corde à linge* – to sleep badly. *Lit.* to sleep on the clothesline.

❄ *passer proche de (faire quelque chose)…* – to come close to (doing something).

❄ *se faire passer un citron* – *sl.* to be handed a lemon, to be handed a dud.

Pas-vite : *adj. & n.m. /fem. –* *sl.* slo-mo, slow (person).

Patate : *n.m. –* potato.

- *bebitte à patates –* cockroach.
- *être dans les patates –* to be in error, to be mistaken. *Lit.* to be in the potato (field).
- *patates frites –* french fries.
- *patates pillées –* mashed potatoes.
- *patates sucrées –* sweet potatoes.
- *Lâche pas la patate !* – Don't give up! *Lit.* Don't let go of the potato.
- *faire patate –* to fail.

Patchée★★ : *adj. –* on the rag, having one's (female monthly) period.

Patcher : *v.t. –* to patch (up), to fix

- *patcher un pneu –* to patch a tire.

Pâte à dents : *n.f. –* toothpaste.

Pâté chinois : *n.m. –* shepherd's pie - an oven-baked pie containing ground beef, corn, and mashed potatoes.

Patente : *n.f. –* thing, object.

- *patente à gosse –* gadget, small object.
- *toute la patente –* the whole bit.

Patenter : *v.t., v.i. –* to patch together, to whip up, to invent.

Patienter : *v.i. –* *Fr.* to wait, to hold on.

On s'excuse de vous avoir fait patienter. – We apologize for the wait.

Patiner : *v.i.* – *Fr.* to skate. Often used to mean "to move" in an allegorical sense.

  ❧ *patiner vite* – to skate quickly (literal and figurative senses).
    Il faut qu'il patine vite s'il veut réussir. – He'd better get a move on if he wants to succeed.
  ❧ *accrocher ses patins* – to end one's career, give up. *Lit.* to hang up one's skates.

Patof : *n.m.* – clown. Originates from a character in a popular 1970's children's TV show.

Patois : *n.m.* – dialect, regional language.

Payer : *v.i./v.t.*- *Fr.* to pay.

  ❧ *payer la traite (à quelqu'un)* – to pay (someone's) way.

Pédaler : *v.i.* – 1. to pedal, or push with one's feet. 2. to make an effort.

  Il faut que tu pédales plus vite si tu veux réussir. – You need to make more of an effort if you want to succeed.
  ❧ *pédaler dans le beurre* – make useless efforts *Lit.* to pedal in butter.

Peinturer : *v.t., v.i.* – to paint.

Pelleter des nuages : *expr.* – to dream (of something unrealistic). *Lit.* to shovel clouds.

Pelure : *n.f.* – *Fr.* skin, outer layer.

  ❧ *enlever une pelure* – to remove one's coat. *Lit.* to take off a layer.

Pend-oreilles : *n.m.* – earring.

Penser : *v.i.* – *Fr.* to think

  ❧ *penser croche* - to think dirty (sexual sense).

Pentré : *n.m.* – kitchen or bathroom counter.

Pépin : *n.m* – inconvenience, problem.

Peppé : *adj.* – psyched, enthusiastic, pepped up.

Péquiste : *n.m./f.* – supporter of the Parti Québécois.

Perdre : *v.t.,v.i.* – *Fr.* to lose.

   ❅ *perdre sa salive* : *expr.* – to waste one's breath. *Lit.* to lose one's saliva.
   ❅ *perdre la track* – to go nuts, to lose one's head. *Lit.* to lose the track.

Peser : *v.t.* – to push, to depress.

   ❅ *peser sur le gaz* – to step on the gas.
   ❅ *Peser sur la suce* – to step on the gas.
   ❅ *peser sur (un bouton)* – to push on (a button).

Pétard : *adj. & n.m./fem.* – knock-out, bombshell (attractive man/woman).

Péter★ : *v.i.* – 1. to fail, breakdown. 2. *Fr.* to pass wind, to fart. 3. to exhaust, to wear out.

   Son char va péter, c'est sûr. – His car is definitely going to break down.
   Ce programme là va pèter le reste du buget. – That program is going to blow the rest of the budget.
   ❅ *Va donc péter dans les fleurs !* – Get outa here, will ya? *Lit.* Go fart in the flowers!
   ❅ *péter de la broue* – to brag about one's abilities. *Lit.* to fart suds.
   ❅ *pèter la balloune* – to fail a breathalyzer (alcohol) test.
   ❅ *se péter les bretelles* – to boast, to brag *Lit.* to snap one's suspenders.
   ❅ *péter une coche* – to blow a fuse, to become furious.
   ❅ *pèter la gueule en sang* – to knock someone's teeth out. *Lit.* to explode one's mouth with blood.

🌿 *péter plus haut que le trou*★ – 1. to live above one's means. 2. to be pretentious. *Lit.* to pass wind above the hole.

Péteux (-euse) de broue : *expr.* – braggart.

Petit change : *n.m.* – loose change.

Petit coin : *n.m* – potty, bathroom. *Lit.* small corner.

(aux) Petits heures : *expr.* – (to) the wee hours of the morning.

Ils se sont laissés aux petits heures. – They parted ways in the wee hours of the morning.

Piasse : *n.f.* – *sl.* buck, dollar. *Def.* piastre.

Piastre : *n.f.* – buck, dollar.

As-tu trois piastres à me passer? – Do you have three bucks you could loan me?

🌿 *avoir des yeux rond comme des piastres* – to have eyes round like saucers.
🌿 *changer quatre trente sous pour une piastre* – 1. to make no profit. 2. to change one thing for another of identical value. *Lit.* to change thirty cents for a quarter.
🌿 *faire le piastre* – to make bucks, to make a lot of money.

Pichou★★ **:** *n.m.* – unattractive woman.

Picosser : *v.i.* – to rummage, to forage.

Picrelle★★ **:** *n.f.* – prostitute, tramp.

Pied : *n.m.* – *Fr.* foot, the length of one foot.

🌿 *être à pied* – to be in financial difficulty.
🌿 *avoir les deux pieds dans la même bottine* – to be clumsy, unresourceful. *Lit.* "to have both feet in the same boot".

Piger : *v.t.* – to get, to grab, to take.

Pigrasser : *v.t.* – to screw around, to waste time.

Pigrasseux (-euse) : *n.m. /f.* – one who wastes time.

Pile : *n.f.* – pile.

Il laisse traîner des piles de ses affaires partout dans la maison. – He leaves piles of his stuff all over the house.

Piler : *v.t., v.i.* – 1. to peel, to scrape off. 2. to walk on, to walk over.

Attention, tu viens de piler sur mes papiers ! – Watch it, you just walked on my papers!

Piment : *n.m.* – pepper (vegetable).

 piment fort – hot pepper.

Pinch : *n.m.* – small beard encircling the mouth.

Piner : *v.i.* – to annoy, to bother, to harrass.

Il me pine là-dessus depuis deux jours. – He's been bothering me for two days about that.

Pinotte : *n.f.* – peanut.

Pinte : *n.f.* – pint.

Pipe : *n.m.* – 1. *Fr.* (smoking) pipe. 2. lie, false story.

Raconte–moi pas de pipes, je sais très bien ce qui est arrivé. – Don't lie to me, I know very well what happened.

Piquer : *v.t.* – to grab, to snatch.

   piquer une crise – to throw a fit.
   piquer une jasette – to have a chat.

Piquetage : *n.m.* – picketing.

Piqueter : *v.i.* – to picket (a place).

Pire : *adj.* – *Fr.* worst, the worst, bad.

   au pire aller – in the worst case.
   c'est pas pire ! – Not bad!
   pas si pire – not so bad.
   (de) pire en pire – worse and worse.
   pas pire, pantoute ! – Not bad, not bad at all!

Pis : *conj.* – 1. and, next. 2. "So?" 3. "What's new?" *Def.* puis.

   Pis toi ? – And you?
   Et pis ? – And so?

Pisse-minute : *n.f.* – someone with a frequent need to visit the bathroom.

Pissou : *n.m.* – fraidy-cat, coward.

Pitcher : *v.t.* – to throw, to pitch.

   Je vais pitcher ça à la poubelle. – I'm going to throw that out.

Piton : *n.m.* – button. (*Impl.* any surface able to be pressed down).

   être de bonne heure sur le piton – to be up at the crack of dawn. *Lit.* to be on the button early.
   mettre la musique dans le piton – to play music at high volume.

Pitonner : *v.i.* – 1. to press a button 2. to channel surf.

Arrête de pitonner, toi ! – Stop changing channels!

Pitonneuse : *n.f.* – remote control (for a TV, etc.).

Pitou : *n.m.* – 1. pooch, dog. 2. child, kid (affectionate).

Pauvre p'tit pitou – Poor little guy.

Pitoune★★ : *n.f. & adj.* – 1. over-dressed, over-made girl. 2. floating log (from lumbering and transporting logs via river). 3. token, bingo chip.

Placer : *v.t., v.i.* – to put, to place.

🔧 *placer un appel* – to place a call.

Placotage : *n.m.* – gossip, chatter.

Placoter : *v.i.* – to gossip, to chatter.

🔧 *placoter sur le dos de quelqu'un* – to talk behind (someone's) back.
Ils n'arrêtaient pas de placoter sur le dos de Yannick. – They gossiped non-stop about Yannick.

Plaisant(e) : *adj.* – nice, pleasant.

Planche : *n.f.* – Fr. board, plank.

🔧 *à planche* – all the way, completely.
On va faire ça à planche. – We'll do it all the way.
🔧 *faire de la planche (à neige)* – to snowboard.

Planification : *n.f.* – planning.

Planifier : *v.t., v.i.* – Fr. to plan, to schedule.

(se) Planter : *v.i.* – to fail.

>*Ça va planter, sûr.* – It's going to fail, for certain.
>*Il va se planter au moment d'essayer.* – He's going to fail as soon as he tries.

Plaster : *n.m.* – band-aid.

Platée : *n.f.* – plateful (of food).

>*Ça, c'est toute une platée !* – That's quite a plateful!

Platte : *adj.* – 1. boring, annoying 2. unfortunate.

>*Je la trouvais pas mal platte, son histoire.* – I found his story pretty boring.
>*C'est platte, ça !* – That's a shame!
>❄ *(une) joke platte* – a stupid joke.

Plein : *adj.* – *Fr.* full.

>❄ *(en) avoir plein son casque* – to have enough. *Lit.* to have one's hat full.

Pleumer : *v.t.* – to pluck (feathers, etc).

>❄ *se faire pleumer* – to get taken, to be had. *Lit.* to get plucked.

Pleurnichard : *adj.* – a cry-baby, easily crying.

Pleuvoir : *v.i.* – *Fr.* to rain

>❄ *Il pleut à boire debout* – It's raining very hard. *Lit.* It's raining to drink standing up.
>❄ *Il pleut des cordes* – It's raining very hard. *Lit.* It's raining cords of wood.

Pli : *n.m.* – fold, pleat.

>❄ *faire un pli* – to be bothered or upset by something. Generally used in the negative: *Ça ne me fait pas un pli* – That doesn't bother me at all.

Plotte★★★ : *n.f.* – 1. slut, whore. 2. reference to female genitalia.

   avoir la plotte à terre★★★ – to be exhausted.

Ploguer : *v.t.* – to plug in, to connect.

Je vais l'ploguer dans le mur. – I'll plug it in the wall.
Il est pas mal plogué dans l'industrie. – He's pretty well connected in the industry.

Pluie verglaçante : *n.f.* – freezing rain.

Plus ou moins : *expr.* – more or less. (generally implies less)

Poche : *adj.* – bad, ugly.

Son dessin était pas mal poche. – His drawing was pretty bad.

Poche : *n.f.* – male sexual organs.

Pocher : *v.t.* – to screw up, to do a bad job (on something).

Poêle : *n.f.* – stove.

Pogner : *v.t., v.i.* – 1. to get, to receive. 2. to grab, to trap, to catch. 3. to have (sense of possession). 4. to quarrel, to argue. 5. to be successful with the opposite sex.

J'ai pogné un rhume. – I caught a cold.
On a été pognés dans la neige pendant deux heures. – We were stuck in the snow for two hours.
C'est fou comment qu'il pogne, ce gars là – It's amazing how well that guy does with women.

   pogner son air – to be surprised. *Lit.* to take (one's) breath.

   se faire pogner – to get caught.

   pogner une chicane – to argue, to have a dispute.

❧ *pogner le jackpot* – to hit the jackpot.
❧ *pogner le Klondike* – to strike it rich, to succeed.
❧ *pogner les nerfs* – to become irritable, angry.
❧ *se pogner le bacon* – to goof off, to do nothing
❧ *se pogner le cul* – to goof off, to do nothing.
❧ *se pogner le derrière* – to goof off, to do nothing

(se) Pogner : *v.i.* – to hook up, to get together (romantically).

Pogné : *adj.* – stuck.

Je suis vraiment pogné là-dessus. – I'm really stuck on that point.

Poignée : *n.f.* – *Fr.* handle.

❧ *avoir une poignée dans le dos* – to be gullible. *Lit.* to have a handle on one's back.

Poil : *n.f.* – *Fr.* hair.

❧ *Bibitte à poil* – small animal.

Pointer : *v.t.* – to point out, to highlight.

Il m'a pointé trois problèmes différents avec la compagnie. – He pointed out three different problems with the company.

Poli à ongles : *n.m.* – nail polish.

Police montée : *n.f.* – mounted police.

Pompette : *adj.* – drunk, intoxicated.

Poque : *adj.* – 1. tired or hurt (for a person) 2. broken (for an object) 3. trashed, very drunk (for a person) .

Possiblement : *adv.* – possibly.

Poteau : *n.m.* – post, telephone pole.

    🍁 *sirop de poteau* – imitation maple syrup. *Lit.* telephone pole syrup.

Potter : *v.t.* – to sink (something).

    🍁 *potter un but* – to make a goal, to sink a puck (hockey)

Poucer : *v.i.* – to hitchhike, to thumb a ride..

Poupoune : *n.f.* – overmade, badly-dressed woman.

Pour : *prép.* – 1. *Fr.* for. 2. according to, as for.

    Pour moi, j'en ai marre. – As for me, I've had enough.

    🍁 *être pour (quelque chose)* – to be in favor of (something), to be all
    for (something).

Pourquoi (que) : *art., pron.* – why (the reason that). *Pourquoi* is often
used directly as a pronoun:

    C'est pourquoi que je suis venu. – That's why I came.

Pourtant : *adv.* – nevertheless, yet.

Pousse-Pousse : *n.m.* – stoller, carriage.

(se) Pousser : *v.i.* – to head out, to take off.

Pousseux(-euse) : *n.m/f.* – hitchhiker.

Poutine : *n.f.* – 1. a mixture of french fries and lumps of cheese covered
in gravy. 2. anything which is a mixture of various elements.

    C'est toute la même poutine. – It's all the same stuff.

(se) Pouvoir : *v.i.* – to be possible, to be thinkable.

> *Ça ne se peut pas qu'il y soit allé !* – There's no way he could've gone!
> ❄ *Ça s'peut-tu que…* – Could it be that…

(se) Practiquer : *v.i.* – to practice.

Prélart : *n.m.* – linoleum.

Prendre : *v.t., v.i.* – *Fr.* to take.

> ❄ *Ça prend (quelque chose) pour…* – (Something) is necessary to…
> ❄ *prendre un break* – 1. to take a break. 2. to stop dating someone temporarily (romantic sense).
> ❄ *prendre une bouchée* – to grab a bite.
> ❄ *prendre une brosse* – go on a bender, to get drunk.
> ❄ *prendre le champs* – to drive off the road. *Lit.* to take to the fields.
> ❄ *prendre tout son petit change* – to take all one's resources, to take great effort. *Lit.* to take all one's spare change.
> ❄ *prendre un coup* – to go drinking.
> ❄ *prendre un cours* – to take a class.
> ❄ *prendre une débarque* – to take a fall.
> ❄ *prendre une fouille* – to take a fall.
> ❄ *(se) prendre pour le nombril du monde*– to believe one's self to be the most important thing. *Lit.* to take one's self to be the bellybutton of the world.
> ❄ *prendre son temps* – to take (one's) time.
> ❄ *prendre une touche* - to take a drag (on a cigarette, etc)
> ❄ *prendre ça aisé* – to take it easy.
> ❄ *prendre une marche* – to go for a walk.
> ❄ *prendre (quelque chose) en note* – to make note of something.
> ❄ *prendre offense* – to take offense.
> ❄ *prendre la part de (quelqu'un)* – to take (someone's) side.

Prérequis : *n.m., adj.* – *Fr.* requirement, prerequisite.

Présentement : *adv.* – *Fr.* currently, right now, presently.

Pressage : *n.m.* – ironing, pressing.

Presser : *v.t.* – to iron, to press.

Proche : *adj.* – *Fr.* near.

> ❊ *passer proche de (faire quelque chose)*… – to come close to (doing something).

Prometteux(euse) : *adj.* – promising, hopeful.

> *Son projet n'avait pas l'air trop prometteux* – His project didn't seem terribly promising.

Prix de liste : *n.m.* – list price.

Problématique : *n.f.* – problematic situation.

> ❊ *vider le problematique* – to get to the bottom of the problem.

(se) Promener : *v.i.* – *Fr.* to walk, to wander.

> ❊ *se promener en bedaine* – to go shirtless.

Prudemment : *adv.* – prudently, with caution.

Pudding chômeur : *expr.* – simple, inexpensive pudding made from flour and brown sugar. *Lit.* unemployed man's pudding.

Pur laine : *adj.* – dyed-in-the-wool. *Lit.* pure wool.

> *Lui, c'est un Québécois pur laine.* – He's a dyed-in-the-wool Québécois.

Q

Quand que : *expr.* – when, whenever.

Quasiment : *adj.* – almost, *sl.* pretty much.

Quatre-par-Quatre : *n.m.* – 4-by-4, light truck.

Quequ' : *expr.* – … and some. *Def.* Quelque chose. Used after numbers to imply an approximate amount:

    Cent quequ'– *adj.* – one hundred and some.
    Ça m'a coûté trois cent quequ' pour réparer mon char. – It cost me three hundred and something to fix my car.

Quequ' chose : *n.m.* – something. *Contr.* quelque chose).

Quequ' part : *adv.* – somewhere. *Contr.* quelque part).

Quéquette★ : *n.f.* – Penis.

    Grosse corvette, petite quéquette ! – *Lit.* Large corvette, small penis. Used for a wealthy but immature person.

Quessé ? : *expr.* – What is it? *Def.* Qu'est-ce que c'est?

Questa ? : *expr.* – What do you have? What's wrong? *Def.* Qu'est-ce que tu as?

Quétaine : *adj.* – tasteless, bad.

    quétaine au boutte – completely tasteless.
    Ces vêtements sont quétaines au boutte – These clothes are completely tasteless

Quêteux(euse) : *n.m./fem. & adj.* – beggar.

Quille : *n.f.* – bowling pin.

   ❧ *jouer aux quilles* – to bowl, to go bowling.

Quitter : *v.i.* - to leave, to head out.

Quoi : *pron.* – *Fr.* what.

   ❧ *de quoi* – something, anything.
     As-tu de quoi à faire ? – Do you have anything to do?

R

Raboudinage : *n.m.* – botched-up work.

Raboudiner : *v.t.* – to botch, to mess up.

Ragoût de pattes : *n.m.* – traditional Québec fare made from pig's feet and beef meatballs in a rich brown stew.

Raide : *adj.* – stiff.

   ❧ *ben raide* – completely, totally. *Lit.* good and stiff.
   ❧ *fou raide* – completely nuts.
   ❧ *fucké ben raide*★★ – completely screwed up.
   ❧ *raide comme une barre* – stiff as a bar.

(se) Ramasser : *v.t.* – to wind up (somewhere), end up (somewhere).

   Après un bout, on s'est ramassés ici. – After a bit, we ended up here.
   ❧ *se faire ramasser* – to be called on the carpet (for something), to get in trouble.

Rang : *n.m.* – 1. *Fr.* rank (of an organization). 2. country road.

Raqué(e) : *adj.* – tired, exhausted, *sl.* destroyed.

Je suis trop raqué pour sortir à soir. – I'm too exhausted to go out tonight.

Raquettes : *n.f.* – (humerous) term for someone's (oversize) feet.

Ras (au) : *adj.* – near, close to.

Rase-trou : *n.m.* – short item of female clothing (such as a skirt) which is at the limit of good taste. *Lit.* scrape-hole.

Ratoureux(euse) : *n.m./fem. & adj.* – wily, sly, crafty.

Rattrapable : *adj.* – able to be caught.

Rayé : *adj.* – scratched, scraped, dinged.

Rayer : *v.t., v.i.* – to scratch, to scrape.

Recevoir : *v.t., v.i.* – *Fr.* to receive.

    recevoir (quelque chose) sur la tomate – be hit by something unexpected. *Lit.* to catch it on the tomato.

Réchauffé : *adj.* – 1. *Fr.* reheated 2. loaded, drunk.

Recherchist(e) : *n.m./f.* – researcher.

Référer : *v.t., v.i.* – to refer, to pass on.

Regarder : *v.t., v.i.* – *Fr.* to look.

    regarder bien pour… – to look good for…
    Ça regarde bien pour demain ! – Everything looks good for tomorrow!

Réguine : *n.f.* – Device or item that doesn't work as expected. *sl.* a lemon.

La tondeuse que j'ai achetée est une vraie réguine, ça fonctionne une fois sur deux. – The lawnmower I bought is a real lemon, it works one time out of two.

Rejet : *n.m. /fem.* – *sl.* loser, *sl.* reject.

Ce gars-là est un rejet. – That guy is a loser.

Rejoindre : *v.t.* – 1. *Fr.* to meet, to come together. 2. to get a hold of, to catch (up with) someone.

Tu peux le rejoindre chez lui. – You can catch him at home.

Remorqueuse : *n.f.* – tow-truck.

Remplissage : *n.m.* – refill.

  ❧ *remplissage gratuit* – free refill.

Renforcir : *v.t.* – to strengthen.

Renipper : *v.t.* – to fix up, to repair.

Mon chum a renippé son char l'été dernier – My boyfriend fixed up his car last summer.

Revirer : *v.i.* – to swing around, to turn around.

  ❧ *(se) revirer sur un trente sou* – to turn on a dime.

Renvoyer : *v.t.* – 1. to send back, to send away. 2. to vomit, to throw up.

J'ai renvoyé le colis le lendemain. – I sent the package back the next morning.

  ❧ *se faire renvoyer* – 1. to be sent away. 2. to lose one's job.

Reseaurage : *n.m.* – networking, social interaction.

Résident(e) : *n.m./fem.* – *Fr.* resident, inhabitant.

Resoudre : *v.i.* – to arrive uninvited.

Restable : *adj.* – livable, decent. *Lit.* stayable.

On a quitté assez vite puisque le bar n'était pas très restable. – We left pretty quickly since the bar wasn't very decent.

Rester : *v.i.* – 1. *Fr.* to stay. 2. to live, to abide in.

On reste à Jonquière en ce moment. – We're living in Jonquière right now.
* *rester assis sur son steak* – to sit on one's butt, to not do anything.

Restituer : *v.t., v.i.* – to vomit.

Retontir : *v.i.* – to arrive uninvited.

Georges a tendance à retontir à l'heure du souper. – George tends to arrive uninvited around dinnertime.

Retourner : *v.t., v.i.* – *Fr.* to return, to revisit.
* *retourner un appel (téléphonique)*– to call back, to return someone's (telephone) call.

Retracer : *v.t.* – to find again, to rediscover.

On n'a jamais pu retracer le même chemin pour retourner. – We were never able to find the way back there.

Revenir : *v.i.* – *Fr.* to return, to come back.
* *revenir à (ses) moutons* – to come back to the subject at hand. *Lit.* to get back to one's sheep.

Revirer : *v.i.* – to turn around, to reverse course.

Je vais revirer vers Montréal. – I'm going to turn back towards Montréal.

Revoler : *v.t.* – to fly apart, to scatter.

Ricaneux(euse) : *n.m./fem. & adj.* – mocking, scoffing.

Rider : *v.t.* – to push (someone) hard, to ride someone.

Rien : *pron.* – *Fr.* nothing.

➤ *Il n'y a rien là.* – It's nothing.

Rince-bouche : *n.m.* – mouth-wash.

Rincer : *v. 8t.* – *Fr.* to rinse.

➤ *se rincer le bec* - to have a drink. *Lit.* To rinse one's beak.

Robine : *n.f.* – *sl.* rotgut, bad-quality alcohol.

Robineux(euse) : *n.m./fem.* – drunkard, bum.

Rondelette : *adj.* - chubby, overweight (used for a girl or woman).

Rondouillette : *n.f.* - chubby, overweight woman

Roteux : *n.m.* – hot dog.

Rôties : *n.m. pl.* – toast.

Rouge : *n.m.* – *Fr.* red.

➤ *voir rouge* – to see red (be angry).
➤ *être dans le rouge* – to be in the red, to be in financial difficulty.

Rouleuse : *n.f.* – hand-rolled cigarette.

Roulotte : *n.f.* – trailer, camper.

    roulotte à patates – mobile food stand selling french fries.

Route pavée : *n.f.* – paved road.

Roux : *n.m.* – russet, brownish-red. Popular women's hair color.

Runnings : *n.m.pl.* – running shoes.

Rushant(e) : *adj.* – hurried, rushing, stressful.

    Mon travail était rushant. – My job was stressfull.

Rusher : *v.i.* – to be in a rush.

S

Sabler : *v.t.* – to sand (using sandpaper).

Sacoche : *n.f.* – handbag, pocketbook.

    sacoche d'école – school bag.

Sacrament! : *expr.* – By all that's holy!

Sacrant : *adj.* – annoying, aggravating.

    au plus sacrant – as quickly as possible.

Sacre : *n.m.* – oath, blasphemy.

Sacrer : *v.i.* – 1. to swear, to curse. 2. to put or place something in a careless manner. 3. not to care.

Il a descendu tous les saints du ciel tant y a sacré. – He swore so much that he brought all the saints down from the heavens.

J'ai sacré ta jupe sur le comptoir. – I threw your dress on the counter.

Je m'en sacre si tu veux pas y aller ! – I don't give a damn if you don't want to go!

- *se faire sacrer à la porte* **–** to be thrown out (of a job).
- *sacrer son camp** – to leave, to head out.
- *sacrer la paix* – to leave (someone) alone.
- *sacrer (quelqu'un) dehors* – to throw (someone) out.
  Pourrais-tu me sacrer la paix, s'il te plaît ? – Could you leave me in peace, please?

Salle de montre : *n.f* – showroom.

Sans-dessein : *adj. & n.m./fem.* – clueless, thoughtless (person).

Saper : *v.i.* – to chew with one's mouth open.

Sapin : *n.m.* – Fr. fir tree.

- *(se faire) passer un sapin* – to be had, to get a bad deal. *Lit.* to be handed a fir tree.

(se) Saucer : *v.t.* – to dip oneself (gradually) in water , to get wet

Saucette : *n.f.* – 1. brief visit. 2. a dip (in a pool, etc.).

- *faire une saucette* – to go for a dip.
  On va faire une saucette dans la piscine. – We're going to take a dip in the pool.

Saut : *n.m.* – jump, start.

　❧ *faire un saut* – to jump, to start.
　　J'ai fait un saut quand il a ouvert la porte. – I jumped when he
　　opened the door.

Sauté : *adj.* – incredible, unbelievable, mind-blowing, nuts. *Lit.* jumped.

　J'ai vu ce film hier, c'est complètement sauté ! – I saw that film yesterday
　– it was just mind-blowing.

Sauter : *v.t.* – *Fr.* to jump, to leap.

　❧ *sauter une coche* – to blow a fuse, to become furious.
　❧ *sauter un gasket* - to blow a gasket, to become furious.

Sauver : *v.t.* – to save, to conserve.

(se) Sauver : *v.i.* – *Fr.* to escape, to leave in a hurry.

　Il va se sauver du party bientôt. – He's going to leave the party soon.

Scalper : *v.t.* – to scalp tickets.

Schnoute★ : *n.f.* – shit.

　❧ *mange de la schnoute !* – eat shit!

Scie à chaîne : *n.f.* – chainsaw.

Scorer : *v.t.* – 1. to score (a goal). 2. *sl.* to score (sexual sense).

Scrammer : *v.i.* – to scram, to leave quickly.

Scrappe : *n.f.* – junk.

　Mon char, c'est de la scrappe. – My car is a heap.
　❧ *cour à scrap*– junkyard.

Scrapper : *v.t.* – 1. to throw out, to trash (something) 2. to crash (while skiing, etc)

J'ai scrappé mon vélo l'autre jour. – I trashed my bike the other day.

Scratcher : *v.t.* – to scratch (something).

S'cuze ! : *expr.* – Excuse me! *Def.* Excuse-moi !

Sécheuse : *n.f.* – drying machine, dryer.

Séchoir : *n.m.* – hair-dryer.

Secousse : *n.f.* – a while, a period of time.

Ça fait une secousse que je n'y suis pas allé. – It's been a while since I've been there.

Seineux(euse) : *n.m./fem.* – *sl.* busy-body.

Sent-bon : *n.m.* – perfume, eau-de-toilette.

Senteux(euse) : *adj. & n.m./fem.* – Curious, nosy, tactless (person).

Sentir : *v.i.* – 1. *Fr.* to feel. 2. to smell

❧ *sentir le swing* – to smell of sweat.

Séparatiste : *n.m./fem., adj.* – one who supports the political separation of Québec from Canada.

Séraphin : *n.m.* – miser.

Serrer : *v.t.* – 1. *Fr.* to squeeze, to tighten. 2. to put away.

Veux-tu me serrer ça – Would you please put that away for me?

Serviable : *adj.* – usable, workable.

Shafter : *v.i./v.t.* – to give (someone) the shaft.to screw over.

Shaker : *v.i.* – to tremble, to shake (from fright, etc.)

Sharp : *adj..* – 1. smart (for a person) 2. nice, appealing, cool, great.

Shiner : *v.t.* – to shine.

   shiner (ses) souliers – to shine one's shoes.

Shipper : *v.t.* – to send, to ship.

Je vais shipper la boîte demain. – I'll ship the box tomorrow.

Shirer : *v.i.* – 1. to shear, to twist sideways. 2. to slide.

Mon char a shiré sur la glace. – My car slid on the ice.

Shooter : *v.t., v.i.* – 1. to send, transmit. 2. to shoot.

Shoote-moi le fichier et je l'imprime. – Shoot me over the file, and I'll print it out for you.

Siffleux : *n.m.* - marmot

Signaler : *v.t.* – 1. to depress a button (on a phone, etc.).

Pour rejoindre le téléphoniste, signalez le 0. – To reach an operator, press 0.

Simonaque : *expr.* – Dammit!

Sirop d'érable : *n.m.* – maple syrup.

Sirop de poteau : *expr.* – imitation maple syrup. *Lit.* telephone pole syrup.

Slaquer : *v.i.* – *sl.* to goof off, to relax.

Sloune : *n.f.* – (beach) sandal.

Smatte : *adj.* – 1. pleasant, nice 2. show-off

✄ *(un) beau smatte* - one who disappoints by his behavior.

✄ *faire son smatte* – to show off.

Soda à pâte : *n.f* – bicarbonate of soda.

Soignable : *adj.* – able to be healed.

Son chien est mort : *expr* - to be done-in, to be finished. *Lit.* His dog is dead.

Songé(e) : *adj.* – clever, brilliant.

Il n'est pas le gars le plus songé du monde. – He's not the most brilliant guy in the world.

Sortir : *v.i.* – *Fr.* to leave, to depart.

✄ *sortir du bois* – to make it out of the woods, to escape trouble.
Je ne peux pas m'en sortir encore. – I can't get out of it yet.

Sou : *n.m.* – cent, penny.

Est-ce que t'as un vingt-cinq sous ? – Do you have a quarter?

✄ *(se) revirer sur un trente sou* – to turn on a dime.

Soubassement : *n.m.* – basement.

Soue : *n.f.* – sty

✄ *soue à cochons* – pigsty.

✄ *ferme ta soue !* – shut your mouth! *Lit.* shut your sty!

Souffler : *v.t.* – to inflate, to blow up.

Je vais souffler les ballons pour les enfants. – I'm going to blow up the balloons for the kids.

⚜ *souffler dans la balloune.* – to take a breathalyzer test. *Lit.* to blow in the balloon.

Souffleuse : *n.f.* – 1. snowblower. 2 snow plow.

Souliers : *n.m. pl.* – (low-cut) shoes.

Soule : *adj.* – *Fr.* drunk.

⚜ *soule comme une botte* – completely wasted, inebriated. *Lit. as drunk as a boot.*

Soûlon(ne) : *adj. & n.m. /fem.* – drunk, intoxicated.

Soupane : *n.f.* – oatmeal.

Souper : *n.m.* – dinner, evening meal.

Sous : *adv.* – *Fr.* below, under.

Quarante degrés sous zéro – Forty degrees below zero.

⚜ *sous l'impression (que)* – under the impression (that).

Sous-contracteur : *n.m.* – sub-contractor.

Sous-marin : *n.m.* – submarine (sandwich).

Sous-plat : *n.m.* – hotplate.

Souverainist(e) : *n.m. /fem., adj.* – One who supports the political separation of Québec from Canada.

Spinner : *v.t.* – to spin (around).

Splitter : *v.t.* – to split, to divide.

Pour la facture, veux-tu la splitter? – As for the check, shall we split it?

Spotter : *v.t.* – to notice, to spot.

On s'est fait spotter tout de suite. – We were noticed right away.

Squeegee : *n.m./fem.* – Adolescent taken to cleaning windshields at stoplights to earn money.

Squeezer : *v.t., v.i.* – to squeeze, to fit.

Stacose (que) : *expr.*– because, since. *Def.* C'est à cause (que).

Staller : *v.i., v.t.* – to stall, to deliberately delay.

Son projet a pas mal stallé. – His project has pretty much stalled.

Stationner : *v.i., v.t.* – to park (a car).

Stationnement : *n.m.* – parking lot.

Steak : *n.m.* – *Fr.* steak, beef.

⁂ *être assis sur son steak* – 1. to sit on one's butt, to be lazy. 2. to be in a comfortable financial position. *Lit.* to be seated upon (one's) steak.

Stepper : *v.i.* – to start or jump (from surprise).

Quand il m'a parlé, ça m'a tellement surpris que j'ai steppé. – When he spoke to me, it surprised me so much that I started.

Stoné : *adj.* – stoned (on drugs).

Straight : *adj.* – conservative, law-abiding, up-front.

S'tu… : *expr.* – Is it that…. *Def.* Est-ce que c'est…

Stuff : *n.m.* – stuff. Different from English, used only to refer to a single object which is of uncountable quality – such as a medicinal cream, a volume of liquid, a powder, etc.

> *T'es-tu coupé? J'ai du stuff à mettre dessus, si tu veux.* – Did you cut yourself? I have some stuff to put on that, if you want.
> *As-tu ajouté dans le punch le stuff que t'as amené?* – Did you add that stuff you brought to the punch?

Suce : *n.f.* – 1. sucker (for an infant). 2. accelerator (in a car).

> ❋ *pèser sur la suce* – to step on the gas.

Sucette : *n.f.* –hickey, red mark left on the skin from a kiss.

Suçon : *n.m.* – lollipop.

Sucrer : *v.t., v.i.* – *Fr.* to sugar, to sweeten.

> ❋ *se sucrer le bec* – to eat, particularly sweets.

Suisse : *n.m.* – squirrel.

Suiveux : *adj. & n.m./fem.* – follower (not a leader)

Supposé : *adj.* – supposed (to).

> ❋ *être supposé de…* – to be supposed to…
> *Elle est supposée y aller.* – She's supposed to go (there).

Supposément : *adv.* – supposedly.

Surprendre : *v.t., v.i.* – to surprise.

Ça me surprend un peu. **–** That surprises me a bit.

Swell : *adj* – well-dressed, chic.

Swinger : *v.i.* – to party, to dance, to have a good time.

Ça va swinger ce soir. – It's gonna be a blast this evening!

⚜ *Ça swingue en grand* – to work beautifully.

Switcher : *v.t., v.i.* – to change, to switch.

Système de son : *expr.* – sound system.

T

Tabagie : *n.f.* – newspaper stand.

Tabarnac : *expl.* – Goddamn! *Lit.* the tabernacle, the place where the Eucharist is kept in a Roman Catholic church.

Table à café : *n.f.* – coffee table.

Table d'hôte : *n.m.* – restaurant's daily special, usually including an appetizer, a main dish, and dessert/coffee. *Lit.* host's table.

Tablette : *adj.* – room-temperature.

Cette bière est pas mal tablette ! – This beer is pretty much room temperature!

Taboire : *expl.* – Hell! (softer form of *Tabarnac*).

C'est une taboire de belle opportunité. – It's one hell of a great opportunity.

T'à l'heure : *expr.* − 1. earlier. 2. later. *Def.* tout à l'heure.

Tannant(e) : *adj.* − boring, annoying.

L'histoire était un peu tannante. − The story was a bit boring.

Tanné (de) : *adj.* − tired of, fed up, bored with (something/someone).

Viens-t'en, chérie, je suis tanné. − C'mon, sweetie, I'm tired of this…

Tanner : *v.t.* − to bore, to make tired of (something).

Tant que… : *Fr.* as for…

⚜ *tant qu'à y être* − insofar as that may be (the case).

Tantôt : *adv.* − 1. before. 2. soon, afterwards. Can be used in either sense, depending on the context or the tense of the verb used:

Je t'appelle tantôt. − I'll call you later.
Tantôt tu m'avais dit que non. − Earlier, you (had) told me no.

Taoin : *n.m.* − simpleton, imbecile.

Tapette : *n.m.* − effeminate man.

Taper : *v.t.* − *Fr.* to tap, to smack, to hit.

⚜ *taper sur les nerfs* − to exasperate, to annoy. *Lit.* to hit on one's nerves.
Il arrêtait pas de me taper sur les nerfs. − He wouldn't stop annoying me.

Taponnage : *n.m.* − hesitation, dallying.

Taponner : *v.i.* − to dally, to beat around the bush.

Arrête de taponner et donne-moi la réponse ! − Stop dallying and give me the answer!

Taponneux(euse) : *n.m./fem., adj.* – one who hesitates or dallies.

Tarla : *n.m.* – idiot, fool.

Tas : *n.m.* – a bunch, a cluster (of something)

Tata : *n.m./fem. & adj.* – imbecile, simpleton.

Tataouinage : *n.m.* – indecision, hesitation.

Tataouiner : *v.i.* – to fool around, to waste time (on unimportant things).

Teigne : *n.m./fem.* – pestering or harrassing person.

Téléroman : *n.m.* – TV series, such as a sitcom or soap opera.

Téléphone : *n.m.* – 1. *Fr.* telephone. 2. telephone call.

J'ai eu un téléphone de lui hier. – I got a call from him yesterday.

Tempête de neige : *n.f.* – snowstorm.

Temps : *n.m.* – *Fr.* time.

- *faire du temps* – to do time (in prison).
- *à temps* – in time.
- *avoir le temps dans sa poche* – to take one's time, to go slowly. *Lit.* to have the time in one's pocket.

   Ne t'inquiète pas, il va arriver à temps. – Don't worry, he'll arrive on time.

Tends : *expr.* – *Def.* Attends.

Tends minute ! – Wait a sec!

Tenir : *v.t. – Fr.* to hold.

> ❧ *tenir à (quelqu'un)* – to care about someone.
> *Je tiens beaucoup à toi* – I care about you a lot.

Tenter : *v.i.* – 1. *Fr.* to try, to attempt. 2. to tempt, to interest.

> *J'ai tenté de le faire tantôt.* – I tried to do it earlier.
> *Est-ce que ça te tente de venir avec nous ?* – Are you interested in coming with us?

Tête : *n.f. – Fr.* head.

> ❧ *avoir la tête à Papineau* – to be very intelligent.
> ❧ *tête de rubber* – numskull, dunce. *Lit.* rubber head.

Téter : *v.i.* – to hesitate.

Téteux(euse) : *n.m./fem. & adj.* – 1. *sl.* boot-licker, brown-noser. 2. hesitant person.

'ti : *Def.– Fr.* petit (small).

> *Je prendrais bien un 'ti café* – I'll take a small coffee.

Tieindre : *v.t., v.i.* – to hold.

Tiguidou : *expr.* – *sl.* okey-dokey.

Tinker : *v.t.* – 1. to fail, *sl.* to tank, *sl.* to go belly-up. 2. to fill up (a tank), *Ex.* that of a car.

> *Son projet va sûrement tinker.* – His project is definitely going to fail.
> *Je vais aller tinker d'abord.* – I'm going to fill up my car first.

Tirer : *v.t. – Fr.* to pull.

- *tirer le diable par la queue* – to be very poor. *Lit.* to pull the devil by the tail.
- *(se) tirer la pipe* – to pull (someone's) leg. *Lit.* to pull the pipe.
- *(se) tirer une bûche* – to join in (a conversation, etc). *Lit.* to pull up a log.

Tizoune : *n.m./fem.* – dunce.

Tomber : *v.i. – Fr.* to fall.

- *tomber en amour* – to fall in love.
- *tomber sur les nerfs* – to exasperate, to annoy. *Lit.* to hit on one's nerves.
  Il arrêtait pas de me tomber sur les nerfs. – He wouldn't stop annoying me.

Toasté : *adj.* – 1. toasted, grilled; 2. drunk.

- *toasté des deux bords.* – completely sloshed, very drunk. *Lit.* toasted on both sides.

Toaster : *v.t.* – 1. to toast 2. to overuse, to burn out.

Tomate : *n.f. – Fr.* tomato

- *recevoir (quelque chose) sur la tomate* – be hit by something unexpected *sim.* "to catch it on the chin". *Lit.* to catch it on the tomato.

Toppe : *n.f.* – cigarette.

Toquant(e) : *adj.* – heavy, filling (for food).

La bouffe était bonne et assez toquante ! – The food was great, and pretty filling.

Torcher : *v.i.* – 1. to move rapidly. 2. to not care (*s'en torcher**). 3. to clean in a rough manner.

> *Y torche, ton char!* – Hey, your car really moves!
> *Je m'en torche s'il vient ou non.* – I don't give a damn if he comes along or not.

Torchon : *n.m.* – rag.

> ❧ *A chaque guenille son torchon* – To every girl her guy. *Lit.* to each cloth its rag.

Tordre : *v.t.* – *Fr.* to twist

> ❧ *tordre le bras (de quelqu'un)* – to twist (someone's) arm, to insist.

Torrieux : *expl.* – Damn!

Torvis : *expl.* – Damn!

Toton : *n.m./fem., adj.* – 1. idiot, fool. 2. (*n.m. Pl.*) *boobs, breasts.*

Touche : *n.f.* - drag, hit (of a cigarette, etc).

> ❧ *prendre une touche* – to take a drag.

Toué : *contr.* – all the... *Def.* "*tous les*".

> ❧ *en toué cas* – in all cases...

Touffe** : *n.f.* – 1. woman of questionable reputation. 2. woman's genital hair.

Toffer : *v.t.* – to put up with (something), to tough (something) out.

> *Ça fait mal, mais je peux le tougher.* – It hurts, but I can take it.

Toune : *n.f.* – Tune, melody.

Tourlou : *expr.* – Toodleoo. Used as "goodbye".

Tourmaline★★ : *n.f.* – 1. woman's hat, usually of large proportions. 2. cow dung.

Tourtière : *n.f.* – meat pie.

Tout(e) : *n.m.* – *Fr.* all, everything.
- *tout le kit* – everything, the whole bit.
- *tout le long* – the entire time.
   On sort ensemble, on se voit deux, trois fois par semaine, tout le kit.
   – Yep, we're going out together – we see each other two three times a week, the whole bit.

Tout croche : *adj., adv.* – 1. bad, badly. 2. dirty, distasteful.

Tu parles espagnol tout croche. – You speak Spanish badly.

Toutoune : *n.f.* – roly-poly woman.

TPS : *n.m.* – Federal sales tax.

Track : *n.m.* – (train) track
- *être à coté de la track* – to be in error, to make a mistake. *Lit.* to be next to the (train) track.
- *perdre la track* – to go nuts, to lose one's head. *Lit.* to lose the track.

Traduisible : *adj.* – able to be translated.

Traîne sauvage : *n.m.* – sled, toboggan.

Traîner : *v.t., v.i.* – *Fr.* to drag, to haul, to tow.
- *se traîner les pieds* – to drag one's feet, to take one's time.

Traîneux(euse) : *n.m./fem.* & *adj.–* 1. slow person. 2. someone who constantly makes a mess (leaving a trail of disorder).

Trâlée : *n.f.* – procession, large quantity of things or people.

Elle est arrivée à l'école avec sa trâlée d'étudiants. – She came to the school with her procession of students.

Tranquillement (pas vite) : *expr.* –slowly, gently.

Trappe : *n.f.* – trap, mouth, yap.

Ferme donc ta trappe ! – Shut your mouth, already!

Trente-sous : *n.m.* – quarter, 25 cent piece. *Lit.* thirty cents.

Trimer : *v.t.* – to trim, to cut.

Trippant(e) : *adj.* – impressive, amazing.

Tripper : *v.t.* – 1. *sl.* to dig something, to find something cool, to really like something. 2. to have a crush on (someone).

Je trippe sur son projet ! – I really dig his project!

Trippeux(-euse) : *n. m/f & adj* – (one who) really enjoys (something).

Trôler : *v.i., v.t.* – to troll, to try and catch someone or something.

Il a pas arrêté de trôler pour un date toute la soirée. – He kept looking for a date the entire evening.

Trou : *n.m.* – 1. *Fr.* hole. 2. *sl.* a dive, a less–than–nice place. 3. *trou de cul*★★ – *Fr.* asshole.

Va pas à ce bar-là, c'est un trou. – Don't go to that bar, it's a dive.

- *avoir le trou de cul en dessous du bras* – *Lit.* to be exhausted. to have one's asshole under the arm.
- *boire comme un trou* – to drink like a fish. *Lit.* to drink like a hole.
- *être dans le trou* – to be in trouble. *Lit.* to be in a hole
- *péter plus haut que le trou*★★ – to be a snob. *Lit.* to fart above the hole.

Trouble : *n.m.* – trouble, problem.

- *Il n'y a pas de trouble !* – No problem!

T'sais : *expr.* – Y'know. *Contr.* tu sais.

Truster : *v.t.* – to have confidence in, to trust.

Tuile : *n.f.* – tile.

Tuque : *n.f.* – winter hat.

- *attacher (sa) tuque (avec de la broche)* – To hang on to your hat, to be ready for something
  Attache ta tuque, on va aller skiier sur la piste difficile après ! - Hang onto your hat, we're going to ski down the difficiult slope next!

Turluter : *v.t., v.i.* – to hum, to sing.

Toutoune : *n.f. & adj.* – small overweight woman.

Twit : *n.m./fem., adj.* – idiot, fool, twit.

- *C'est un beau twit !* – He's a complete idiot!

U, V

Ustensiles : *n.m. pl.* – *Fr.* utensils, cutlery.

Vaisseau : *n.m.* – (big) cook pot.

Valise : *n.m.* – 1. *Fr.* suitcase. 2. trunk (of a car).

Valeur : *n.f.* – *Fr.* value.

    être d'valeur – to be a shame, to be unfortunate.
      C'est d'valeur, mais on est déjà pris. – Unfortunately, we're already busy.

Varger : *v.t.* – to strike with force.

    Il était tellement fâché qu'il a vargé dans le mur. – He was so angry that he hit the wall.

    C'est pas vargeux - It's not very strong, it's not brilliant.

Vatendon : *expr.* – "Go on then!" "You're kidding me!" (*Def.* Va t'en donc.)

Vedg : *adj.* – vegged-out, relaxed, at ease.

    Man, je suis complètement veg. – Man, I'm totally vegged out.

Vedger : *v.i.* –

    Je n'ai rien fait tout la journée – j'ai vedgé sur le divan – I didn't to anything all day – just vegged out on the sofa.

Veiller : *v.i.* – to spend the evening, usually at someone's house.

    On va veiller chez lui ce soir. – We're spending the evening at his place.

Veilleux(euse) : *n.m. /fem. + adj.* – one who likes to go to bed very late.

Vente : *n.f.* – *Fr.* sale.

 🦌 *vente de garage* – garage sale.
 🦌 *vente de trottoir* – sidewalk sale

Venter : *v.i.* – to be windy.

Venteux : *adj.* – windy.

Ventiler : *v.i.* – 1. to air out. 2. *sl.* blow off steam, to vent (one's anger).

Versatile : *adj.* – multi-talented, skilled in several fields.

Veston : *n.m.* – suit jacket.

Viande hachée : *n.f.* – smoked meat.

Viarge★★ : *expl.* – Goddamit! *Lit.* Virgin – allusion to the Virgin Mary.

Vidanges : *n.f. pl.* – garbage, trash.

Vidangeur : *n.m.* – garbage man.

Vider : *v.t, v.i..* – *Fr.* to empty

 🦌 *vider le problematique* – to get to the bottom of the problem.

Vignenne : *n.m/f & adj* – (one who is a) rascal, rebel.

Virailler : *v.i.* – 1. to circle, to circumnavigate. 2. to toss and turn in bed.

On a viraillé dans le voisinage pendant une demi-heure, mais on n'a pas pu trouver sa maison. – We circled the neighborhood for half an hour, but couldn't find his house.

Virer : *v.i.* – to turn.

✿ *virer de bord* – to turn around.
✿ *virer fou* – *sl.* to go nuts, to go out of one's mind.
✿ *virer sur le top* – to become the best.

Viser : *v.t., v.i.* – *Fr.* to forsee, to predict.

Je vise que ça pourrait prendre une bonne semaine. – I'd say it could take a good week.

Visionner : *v.t.* – to watch. (a film, a movie, etc)

Visite : *n.f.* – visitors. Generally used in the partitive (*de la visite*), when referring to houseguests.

✿ *avoir de la visite* – to have house guests/company.

Vitement : *adv.* – quickly.

Votation : *n.f.* – voting.

Vous autres : *pron.* – *sl.* y'all, you all.

Voûte : *n.f.* – vault, safe-box.

Voyage : *n.m.* – trip, voyage.

✿ *avoir son voyage* – to have had enough, to be fed up.
C'est la denière fois que je passerais une soirée chez eux – j'ai mon voyage! - That's the last time I'll spend the evening at their place – I've had enough!

Voyons donc! : *expr.* – "C'mon!" "I don't believe it!" *Lit.* Let's see then.

Voyons donc! Je veux te voir! – C'mon! I want to see you!

Vues : *n.f. pl.* – movies.

    ❧ *aller aux vues* – to go to the movies.

W

Wack : *n.m.* – shout, yell.

    ❧ *lâcher un wack* – to let out a yell.

Watcher : *v.t.* – to oversee. *Sl.* to keep an eye on (something/someone).

Wo ! (là) : *expr.* – "Stop!", "That's enough!"

X, Y

Yâble : *n.m.* – devil (*Def. Diable*).

Yeule : *n.f.* – mouth (*Def.* gueule).

Yeux : *n.m. pl.* – *Fr.* eyes.

    ❧ *avoir des yeux (tout) croches* – to have squinty eyes.
    ❧ *avoir les deux yeux dans le même trou* – to be exhausted, i.e. to be staring at a point in space. Lit. to have both one's eyes in the same hole.

Yinque : *expr.* – only. *Def.* Il n'y a que.

Z

Zarzaille : *adj.* – idiotic, foolish.

Zézine★ : *n.f.* – penis.

Zigner : *n.m.* – cf. zigonner.

Zigonnage : *n.m.* - fooling around, stupidity.

Zigonner : *v.i.* – 1. to attempt without much success. 2. to fool around, to waste one's time.

Zigoune : *n.f.* – cigarette (butt).

Ziper : *n.m.* – zipper.

Ziper : *v.t.* – to zip (up).

Il faudrait ziper ton manteau - You'd better zip up your jacket.

Zozo : *adj.* – idiotic, foolish.

Bibliography

Printed Sources

Bélanger, Mario, *Petit guide du Parler québécois*, Les éditions internationales Alain Stanké, 1997.

Béliveau, Marcel, *Savoureuses expressions québécoises*, éditions du Rocher, 2000.

Bergeron, Léandre, *Dictionnaire de la langue québécoise*, Typo, 1997.

Bertrand, Guy, *400 Capsules linguistiques*, Lanctôt éditeur, 1999.

Corbeil, Pierre, *Le Québécois... pour mieux voyager*, éditions Ulysse, 1999.

Côté, Jean, *Expressions populaires québécoises*, Quebecor, 1995.

Denœu, François, *French Idioms*, Barron's Educational Series, 1996.

DesRuisseaux, Pierre, *Dictionnaire des expressions québécoises*, Hurtubise HMH, 1980.

DesRuisseaux, Pierre, *Dictionnaire des proverbes québécois*, Typo, 1997.

DesRuisseaux, Pierre, *Trésor des expressions populaires*, Fides, 1998.

Dubé, Gilberte, *Dictionnaire des expressions imagées*, Les éditions internationales Alain Stanké, 1998.

Dugas, André / Bernard Soucy, *Le dictionnaire pratique des expressions québécoises*, Logiques, 2000.

Dulude, Yvon, *Dictionnaire des injures québécoises*, Les éditions internationales Alain Stanké, 1996.

Durand, Marc, *Histoire du Québec*, Imago, 1999.

Forest, Jean, *Anatomie du parler québécois*, Triptyque, 1996.

Gaborieau, Antoine, *La langue de chez nous*, Éditions des Plaines, 1999.

Gouvernement du Québec, *Le français au Québec*, Conseil de la langue française, 2000.

Keith-Ryan, Heather, *Quebec : Bonjour, eh ?*, Sheltus & Picard, Inc. & VOA Publications Reg'd, 1998.

Mansion, J. E., *Heath's Standard French and English Dictionary*, DC Heath & Company, 1939.

Meney, Lionel, *Dictionnaire québécois français*, Guérin éditeur, 1999.

Proteau, Lorenzo, *Le français populaire au Québec et au Canada*, Les publications Proteau, 1991.

Proteau, Lorenzo, *La parlure québécoise*, Les éditions des amitiés franco-québécoises, 1996.

Scheunemann, Britta, *Le québécois de poche*, Assimil, 1998.

Tétu de Labsade, Françoise, *Le Québec un pays une culture*, Boréal, 1990.

On-Line Sources

Angelfire

http://www.angelfire.com/pq/lexique/lexique.html

Notes